HEALING
with the

Fairies

HEALING
with the

Fairies

Messages, Manifestations,
and Love From the
World of the Fairies

Doreen Virtue, Ph.D.

HAY HOUSE, INC.
Carlsbad, California
London • Sydney • Johannesburg
Vancouver • Hong Kong

Published and distributed in the United States by: Hay House, Inc., P.O. Box 5100, Carlsbad, CA 92018-5100 • *Phone:* (760) 431-7695 or (800) 654-5126 • *Fax:* (760) 431-6948 or (800) 650-5115 • www.hayhouse.com • *Published and distributed in Australia by:* Hay House Australia Pty. Ltd., 18/36 Ralph St., Alexandria NSW 2015 • *Phone:* 612-9669-4299 • *Fax:* 612-9669-4144 • *e-mail:* info@hayhouse.com.au • *Published and Distributed in the United Kingdom by:* Hay House UK, Ltd. • Unit 62, Canalot Studios • 222 Kensal Rd., London W10 5BN • *Phone:* 44-20-8962-1230 • *Fax:* 44-20-8962-1239 • *Distributed in Canada by:* Raincoast • 9050 Shaughnessy St., Vancouver, B.C. V6P 6E5 • *Phone:* (604) 323-7100 • *Fax:* (604) 323-2600B.C. V6P 6E5 • *Phone:* (604) 323-7100 • *Fax:* (604) 323-2600

Editorial supervision: Jill Kramer • *Design:* Summer McStravick

Library of Congress Cataloging-in-Publication Data

Virtue, Doreen
    Healing with the fairies : how nature's angels can help you in every area of your life / Doreen Virtue.
        p. cm.
    ISBN 1-56170-807-0 (tradepaper)
    1. Fairies. I. Title.

BF1552 .V57 2001
133.1'4—dc21

2001016778

ISBN 13: 978-1-56170-807-9
ISBN 10: 1-56170-807-0

08 07 06 05   12 11 10 9
1st printing, May 2001
9th printing, January 2005

Printed in Canada

❀ ❀ ❀

To God,
and the wondrous fairies, dolphins,
mermaids, ascended masters, and angels.
My heart overflows with gratitude
for all of your help!

❀ ❀ ❀

Contents

PREFACE

The Truth about Fairies

Like most children, I had a favorite book of bedtime stories. But it wasn't the stories within the pages of the book that captured my young fancy. Rather, it was the painting on the book's cover. I'd stare endlessly at the fantastically detailed illustration of purple-and-white morning glory lilies.

Each flower in the painting was home to a beautiful, tiny fairy who lived among the flowers in the same way that you and I live among houses, stores, and office buildings. It was their city, their home, and their community.

I've always loved gazing at fairy portraits, but it wasn't until I reached adulthood that I began actively working with the fairy realm. Perhaps I did unknowingly, though, during my childhood when I played in the field behind my home.

It's interesting that I always believed in angels, but my understanding of fairies came later in life. I suspect that this same transition is true for many adults. As usual, this shift was in Divine and perfect order for my current assignment, in which I was asked to teach about the reality of fairies.

It's a fact that most people love angels. Up to 80 percent of us believe that angels are real. However, a considerably smaller percentage of us believe that *fairies* are real, live beings. Instead, they are merely regarded as fodder for fictional tales—and, of course, there's always the tooth fairy. There are also those who consider fairies to be symbols of dark occult worship. Christian communities sometimes don't understand that fairies are part of God's wondrous creation—a branch of the angelic realm that is assigned to watch over plants, animals, and the earth as a whole.

Still others think that fairies aren't trustworthy, but are mischievous imps who hide objects or cause dire harm. The truth is that fairies are here to improve and extend the lives of all beings, including us humans. No one is suggesting that we *worship* fairies or angels—the fairies and angels give all glory to the Creator. Since God's love and light is omnipresent, humans, angels, and fairies are all joined as One.

The Living Spirit World

During the process of fearlessly looking at the spirit world with my sense of clairvoyance wide open, I saw many so-called mythical creatures, with lives just as real as ours. I learned rapidly that we are all God's sparks of Divine light on the inside. However, there are many different forms and levels that we sparks can assume.

Each Divine spark that incarnates lives on a specific level of the astral plane. The humans live on the densest energy level, followed by the plants and animals, who are more spiritually attuned than most humans. The fairies and the other elementals live on the astral-plane level just above the animals and the plants, so they are half incarnated, and half in the spirit world.

Deceased loved ones live on the plane slightly above the fairy realm, followed by the ascended masters. The angelic kingdom is on the highest astral-plane level, with the lowest amount of density among the spiritual beings who help us here on Earth.

My teachers in the angelic realm told me about the fairy kingdom. Far from being fictitious creations who populate the world of fairy tales, these beings are very real, powerful, and loving. Fairies are God's guardian angels of nature, and they ensure the health and safety of animals, plants, and Mother Earth. In that respect, they also play a significant role in helping and directing us humans. Fairies can also bring a sense of magic, playfulness, and romance into our lives.

The fairies' existence reminds me of the Dr. Seuss story "Horton Hears a Who," where a race of beings known as the "Whos" live on a dandelion that is threatened with destruction. The Whos will become extinct unless someone can save the dandelion.

One small child hears the Whos' cries and tries to get others to help save them, but no one believes the child's contention that the Whos are a real, live race of beings. Finally, the Whos collectively sing loudly enough so that everyone hears them and become convinced that the dandelion really is populated. Their planet and race is saved!

In the same way, the fairies' existence is threatened because we don't believe in them. We destroy their homelands every time we kill a wild plant or tree, and we cause them to suffer with our toxic pesticides and cleaning supplies. The fairies, unlike the angels, have a physical body. It is a very light, etheric body, yet it has many of the same needs as a human body.

The Fairies' Mission

The fairies are also highly "clairsentient," which means that they are emotionally and physically sensitive to the thoughts and emotions of others. Fairies are so sensitive that they absorb the pain inflicted upon plants, trees, and animals. They are nature's guardian angels, and they aren't happy unless they are fulfilling this purpose. Also, the fairies need *us* in order to fulfill their purpose.

The fairies want us to be co-guardians of the planet, and the greatest way to get to know the fairies is to be good to planet Earth. For instance, when you go for a walk, bring along a bag to pick up litter along the way. Be diligent about recycling, rinsing out your cans and bottles before throwing them into a recycling bin. Buy and eat as much organic food as possible—to avoid supporting the pesticides that harm our environment and disrupt the fairies (imagine the expression on a fairy's face when she's forced to breathe bug spray!).

At first when working with the fairies, you will sense them in a breeze blowing through the leaves, while inhaling the scent of flowers, or in the fragrance of the lawn and soil. You'll revel in the fairies' presence when you gaze upon moonlit bushes, or stare at newborn flower buds. In time, as you and the fairies get to know each other, they become increasingly visible.

I was delighted to discover how wonderful we can feel around the fairies. Just being in a fairy's presence can make us feel euphoric, lighthearted, playful, and generally happy inside. The fairies can also help us find our heart center. They are naturally gifted healers who can assist us in releasing fear and darkness from our lives.

❦ ❦ ❦

[**Editor's Note:** In the upcoming text, to differentiate between the fairies' and angels' messages—and Doreen's mentally projected responses—the former are set in italics *with* quotation marks; the latter in italics *without* quotation marks.]

Acknowledgments

A bouquet of gratitude to Grandma Pearl, Steven Farmer,
Nancy Sweatt, Glenn Jaffrey, Nancy Chien-Eriksen,
Charles Schenk, Grant Schenk, Nicole Farmer,
Cat Farmer, Johnna Michelle, Steve Allen, Steve Prutting,
Bronny Daniels, Louise L. Hay, Reid Tracy, Jill Kramer,
Christy Salinas, Jeannie Liberati, Ron Tillinghast,
Shannon Todd, and Summer McStravick.

❧ ❧ ❧

CHAPTER 1

Back
to Nature

"*Go for long walks outdoors.*" I'd heard this sentence in my mind for days now, especially as I climbed on my treadmill to run four miles from the comfort of my bedroom. I'd watch the red LED lights counting down my 45-minute workout, and all I could hear was, *"Go do this outside!"*

Little did I know that some very special angels—those assigned to nature—were trying to get my attention. Their persistent chant finally paid off, and one sunny Wednesday afternoon, I bypassed the treadmill in favor of the sidewalk.

I walked along Selva Avenue in Dana Point, California, the seaside town located midway between Los Angeles and San Diego where I lived. Selva Avenue has long and hilly sidewalks leading to Salt Creek Beach. As the traffic on Golden Lantern Boulevard whizzed by, I wondered why I was called to walk outdoors. *This seems stressful, compared to working out in the quiet setting of my own bedroom,* I mused.

So, the next day when the fairies urged me to go for an outdoor walk, I took along my Sony Walkman, hoping that turning up the volume on my cassette tape of *A Course in Miracles* would drown out the traffic noise.

Co-writing with Spirit

It was the spring of 1997. I had just finished writing *The Lightworker's Way*, a book that I wrote in complete isolation. I'd taken the phone off the hook for three and a half months and had told all my friends and associates that I would see them when the book was done. During the process of writing, the angels were very specific in their instructions. They told me to stay in a state of centered meditation, keep fresh stargazer and tuber roses nearby, use soft lighting, and listen to classical music. They also urged me to keep my mind off worldly affairs, and focus on the truth of peace and love.

While the isolation was difficult, I saw immediate results from following the angels' advice. My office felt like an ashram, a sacred cave where the energy was high and pure. *The Lightworker's Way* seemed to reflect that high-frequency energy and intention, and to this day, it remains one of my favorite authored books.

I was now in the midst of writing a new book called *Angel Therapy*. The whole project felt oddly "directed," as if the angels knew exactly what the book would be and do. Even the planned publication of *Angel Therapy* seemed surreal. In the past, my publisher had always requested that I submit a detailed book proposal. Yet in this case, I had simply e-mailed them three sentences, mentioning that I'd like to write a book called *Angel Therapy*, with a brief description. My publisher immediately said, "Yes!" and sent a book contract without questions about its format, length, or other details.

The writing of the book was odd, too. I seemed to enter into a trance whenever I'd sit down to write. Completely unaware of what words were coming through my fingers onto the keyboard, I was practically afraid to read the text afterward. Part of me feared that it would be unintelligible and I'd have to start writing all over again. I was also aware that the process of trance-channeled writing triggered my "control issues." Surrendering and trusting completely wasn't natural for me—perhaps a product of my head-strong Taurean nature, or maybe a result of being a first-born child.

Nevertheless, I was quite aware of the spirit world's instructions. I never doubted their validity; I only hesitated in following them. Ever since a carjacking incident on July 15, 1995, in which I'd ignored my angels' warning and narrowly escaped theft, and perhaps, death, I'd done my best to heed heaven's advice. Yet, despite my brush with near-disaster (which I'll explain more fully later on), my ego would still occasionally kick in and argue with my angels.

While writing *Angel Therapy*, the angels acted like Olympic coaches, advising and motivating me toward optimum performance. They clearly wanted *Angel Therapy* written and released. So, I thought the urgings to go for outdoor walks were just part of the process. It turned out, though, that I was being prepared for work they foresaw me doing in the future: the book you are currently holding in your hands.

Connecting with Nature

I walked briskly along Selva Avenue, listening to the pleasant male voice narrating *A Course in Miracles* through my headphones. Oblivious to anything but his words and my footsteps, I might have missed an extraordinary sight, but the intense color of some purple bougainvillea flowers in front of me stopped me in my tracks. I turned off the cassette to give the flowers my full attention. Never before had I seen a hue this vibrant. The bluish-purple was so dazzling that I couldn't get enough of it.

I put my face as close as possible to the flowers, hoping to quench my eyes' thirst for the luscious color. Still, it wasn't enough; I felt as if I wanted to consume and merge with the glowing hues. I walked to the next bougainvillea tree along the sidewalk, and the next, and the next. Nearly an hour passed, while I stood transfixed amid the blossoms that looked like purple moths sitting atop green leaves.

As I tore myself away from my new friends, I was amazed that I hadn't even noticed the traffic noise. My connection with nature had been so profound that time and sound ceased to exist. And that's when I simultaneously began my connection with the nature angels—the fairies and elementals—although I wouldn't realize it for quite some time.

The next day, some inner sense compelled me to leave my cassette player at home. I knew that the angels were asking me to open my ears so I could hear them fully. My inner voice guided me to pack a blank notebook and a reliable pen, along with my house key and water bottle. I retrieved a green-and-pink hip pack from my closet that I'd been given as a guest on the *Leeza* show years earlier, and put my notebook in it (covered with a small plastic sandwich bag to waterproof it lest an errant ocean wave erase the messages I knew that I'd pen).

The writing on *Angel Therapy* had gone especially well the previous evening. Usually I'd only been able to withstand channeling for 15 to 30 minutes without getting a headache, but last night I'd been able to channel for nearly two hours. Had my encounter with the bougainvillea helped?

When I'd asked the angels why I got headaches during my channeling sessions—after all, I had never been prone to them before—they'd told me that my steady diet of chocolate was interfering with my energetic vibrational frequencies.

In other words, my "antennae" couldn't connect with the high frequencies of the angelic realm, because chocolate was making me dense and slow. I had been aware that chocolate was a poor substitute for human love, and that we often craved it when we really wanted romantic love, but now the angels were explaining to me that chocolate cravings were really a desire for God's love—a yearning to connect with our Creator.

When we eat chocolate, we fill in the neuron receptors that are designed for Divine love with the synthetic chemicals called "phenelethylamine," or P.E.A., for short—a fitting name, since "pea" is a small substitute for the grand love that can only be filled when our hearts are in love with our Creator and all of Creation.

Yet, I was the quintessential chocoholic, and I mentally argued with the angels. After all, my third book, *The Chocoholic's Dream Diet*, was all about chocoholism! I craved and ate chocolate daily, even though I'd switched to "healthier" versions of the "drug," such as chocolate soy milk, chocolate rice "ice cream," and chocolate "health bars."

If you want me to give up chocolate, you're going to have to remove my cravings! I practically yelled at my angels. I'd

5

learned that our angels appreciate us being honest and authentic with them, and aren't offended when we express genuine emotions. So, during those moments of exasperation when I'd wondered how I could possibly follow Divine guidance—that is, giving up chocolate—my angels were accustomed to my indignant tone. Angels focus only on the love they see within us, and not on our fears, which trigger anger and distrust.

My request that the angels heal my chocolate cravings was half rhetorical and half said in earnest. Could the angels really remove a lifelong addiction to a fattening stimulant? I had my answer the next day. As if the angels had worked on me throughout the night, by morning I was free of all chocolate cravings. *I haven't wanted, and haven't eaten, chocolate since that day!*

This was no minor feat for the former "Queen of Chocolate," my self-imposed title. Many of my audience members, students, and readers, knowing of my story, have reported similar results after asking their angels for assistance with chocolate and other types of addictions.

Almost immediately, I could channel passages of *Angel Therapy* for longer periods of time, free of headaches or other physical discomfort. As I thought about this during my walk, I heard the angels say, *"All food affects you, long after it is digested."* I stopped and wrote this phrase in the little notebook in my hip pack. *So, the angels are going to instruct me during my walks in nature!* I thought. *No wonder they don't want me distracted by listening to an audiotape! I am here to listen and take notes.*

That day as I sat on the foggy beach with pen in hand, the angels explained the effects of food on our spiritual psyche, information I've written about in my books *Divine Prescriptions* and *Eating in the Light*.

I still had little awareness that a branch of the angelic kingdom known as "the elementals" was counseling me. These beings are the doctors, nurses, and counselors assigned to help and heal all Earthly beings (including humans). Fairies are one type of elemental, and you'll meet other members of the elemental kingdom throughout this book. To me, anyone who helps us is an "angel," and elementals definitely help us. In my own case, though, I had no idea to what extent the fairies and other elementals were assisting me, and how much they were a part of my life.

Nature's Angels

I kept up my daily walks, taking notes and doing trance-channeled writing for *Angel Therapy*. For the second half of the book, the angels dictated material about the "nature angels," and they taught me—as well as my readers who were unfamiliar with them—about interacting with the fairies. I learned that animals' guardian angels are fairies, and that they also work closely with flowering plants.

As I read the angels' words, I glanced at my Himalayan cat, Romeo, and noticed glowing lights around him. I gasped with delight and surprise, and quickly looked at the stargazer lily bouquet in my office. It had never before occurred to me to look for fairies! But there they were—little Tinkerbells flitting from flower to flower like beautiful fireflies. I half saw them in my mind's eye, and half with my physical sight, similar to how I see angels, deceased people, and auras. My spiritual and physical sight meld together to give me one unified vision of the spirit world, which I see with my physical eyes open.

The angels—or was it the fairies, I now wondered—

channeled more information for the "Nature Angels" chapter of *Angel Therapy*. They said that we humans should be cautious when walking on or mowing grass, and should offer mental warnings to the fairies so that they can scurry out of the way of feet and lawnmowers. They also warned against using pesticides, as poisons are as noxious to fairies as they are to insects.

They explained that fairies have a type of physical body, so environmental pollutants and human carelessness affect them. All spiritual beings—whether human, animal, fairy, deceased person, or angel—have a body composed of energy and "light matter." This light matter has a form that gives it shape and mass. The consciousness, or thought pattern, of the being determines the density of a person's energy. Humans have the densest, most concrete, opaque bodies, because our thoughts are largely materially focused. We think heavy thoughts, and our bodies reflect this consciousness.

The angels said that because we humans do things the hard way, such as silently enduring a job we can't stand instead of using the power of thought, prayer, and manifestation, we have dense bodies that are masses of hardened thoughts about materiality.

The elemental kingdom, in contrast, regularly uses manifestation to attract or create their needs. This gives them lighter hearts and schedules, and thus, their bodies are lighter than ours. Nonetheless, the fairies' mind-sets are denser than angels, who are completely focused upon Spirit. To the angels, Jesus' words, "Seek ye first the kingdom of God, and all this shall be added unto you," are the guiding words that will lift us from density, suffering, and hardship.

The angels then told me something that immediately rang true, yet which still surprised me: *"Your human bodies are elementals. They have a life force and intelligence all their own, coming from the elemental kingdom."* The angels explained that our body has a natural intelligence, which regulates its systems, yet it also can have the impetuous personality of a two-year-old child.

This child within the body—the being that demands and craves both the healthful and the unhealthful—is the elemental within all of us. The body is a separate individual being, with its own mind, life force, and life plan. We don't own the body, and it isn't an extension of us. It is essentially a roommate with whom we have a synergistic and mutually dependent relationship. We depend upon the body to house and transport "us," the soul; and the body depends on us to feed, shelter, and exercise it. The body's origin is of the spirit world, yet it is a dense being of the earth. Bodies are, therefore, part of the Earth kingdom of angels—the elemental realm, in other words. The body is our inner fairy, leprechaun, unicorn, mermaid, or one of the other members of the elemental kingdom.

So, our bodies are elementals! I marveled at the realization. They are denser bodies than the wispy, etheric bodies of the fairies, but our bodies are definitely in the same family. No wonder the fairies are brilliant healers of human bodies— they are merely working on their relatives when they work on our bodies. Just being out in nature, and holding the intention to connect with the fairies, can have a physical healing effect.

❦ ❦ ❦

CHAPTER 2

The Heart Chakra

I was acutely aware of the elemental realm within my body that evening as I made dinner for my husband, Michael; my son Grant; and myself. As I arranged "Hav'a Chips" (a healthful brand of corn chips) across the bottom of each dinner plate, I was tempted to start munching on them, yet I recognized the urge to binge as coming from my elemental body. Like a two-year-old, my body was demanding instant pleasure and gratification. Just my awareness of its demanding nature helped me. Inwardly, I told it, *You'll have plenty to eat in just a moment,* and my words quelled my body's cravings instantly.

Just then, Grant, who was 16 at the time, and my cat, Romeo, sauntered into the kitchen. Apparently they were hungry, too. Grant asked, "Is dinner just about ready?," and Romeo echoed the same question with his, *"Meow!"* My sweet cat affectionately nuzzled my leg and purred as I opened a can of food for him.

I looked at Romeo and Grant, and almost gasped as I realized how much they both meant to me. Grant, my youngest child, had become so tall and handsome. He had always been such an easygoing person, right from babyhood—and now he was proving to be an exceptional student, as well as a young man with a big heart and high integrity. Recently, Dana Hills High School had awarded him a plaque as a top student in History Studies. I loved and honored him so much!

And Romeo, my beautiful Himalayan cat, with his ocean-colored eyes and winning personality, was the most affectionate animal I'd ever known. Wasn't that why he melted my heart the day I'd adopted him as a small kitten? Romeo cuddled in the crook of my arm and purred at me with those big blue eyes. How could I have ever resisted him?

Gazing at Grant and Romeo, I painfully realized that— as much as I loved them—my heart wasn't fully open to the experience of *feeling* love for them. I understood that I was guarding myself against emotional pain by not fully allowing myself to feel love. Oh sure, I could say, "I love them so much," but I wasn't simultaneously bursting with the *sensation* of love.

"You are afraid of love," the angels told me just then. Their words seemed to stop time, with Grant and Romeo motionless in a freeze-frame. I silently protested the angels' words, embarrassed by their truth.

"Don't be ashamed," they continued. *"All humans fear the*

pain associated with relationships. The fear of being loved, and of giving love, is a human epidemic.

"Unfortunately, this fear of love is the fear of God and the fear of your true self, since you and God are love. When you guard against feeling loved or loving, you are literally guarding against being yourself. You disconnect from your spiritual gifts, which are miraculous, you can be sure. We can assist you in reopening your heart to love, if you will allow us."

Oh, please help me! I want to feel the emotion of love deeply in my heart! I implored the angels mentally. I realized how blunted my emotions were in all of my relationships—in my marriage, with my two sons, with my parents, my friends, and even with my cat. How had I allowed this to happen?

I thought back to all of the times when I'd felt pain associated with "love." It wasn't love in the true spiritual sense of the word, but in the Earthly, relationship sort of love. All of the betrayal and disappointment I'd felt over the years had formed a caked-on crust over my heart. While this crust protected me from deep pain, it also "protected" me from profound joy. I had imprisoned myself in a cell of lukewarm emotions.

Clearing the Heart

After dinner, the angels guided me to my bookshelf, where I picked up *Living a Life of Joy*, an old book by John Randolph Price, one of my favorite authors. Years earlier, his *Abundance Book* had helped me heal my insecurities about money and, thus, my financial life as a whole. Now the angels showed me this book, which contained a key to unlocking my heart and emotions, a process called The Forgiveness Inventory.

I knew from my studies of the spiritual text *A Course in Miracles* that "forgiveness is the key to happiness." I had done my best to practice forgiveness on myself and others as soon as I became aware of resentment or blame. As a psychotherapist, I had encouraged clients to release old anger by forgiving the people and situations in their past. I realized that we often resist forgiving because it threatens the ego. "I won't forgive, because what happened to me is unforgivable," the ego contends. (I actually prefer the phrase, "Release toxins associated with past events and people," rather than the moralistic-sounding admonishment, "Forgive.")

The Inventory instructions asked me to write down the name of every person, situation, and (even) animal who had ever irritated me. I was amazed that I easily wrote four pages, including names of childhood friends I hadn't thought of in years. Sometimes I couldn't remember the name of the person who had irked me, so I'd write a general description of that individual. (Of course, my own name was on the list.) Next, the Inventory asked me to look at each name on the list and then mentally direct the sentiment: *I forgive you. I release you. I hold no unforgiveness back. I am free and you are free.*

I felt physical tingles with respect to each person whom I fully released. For some of my more "challenging" relationships, the releasement exercise felt like a huge whoosh of air shooting out from my heart and head. It was similar to a child who's willfully holding their breath as part of a temper tantrum and then lets it out in one forceful blast.

I felt warm relaxation envelop me as I forgave each person on the list, but I realized that some of the individuals seemed a little more difficult to release. For instance, a part of me still felt frightened by my ex-husband, and another part of me felt vengeful toward the ex-high school boyfriend who'd cheated on me.

The angels taught me that it wasn't as important to forgive the action involved, as it was to see the Godlike innocence within each being. They taught me to acknowledge that everyone makes mistakes—sometimes very painful ones—but that I needed to see the Divine light within myself and within each other person nonetheless. Sometimes this was easy, but other times I'd have to visualize the person in a helium balloon, floating away from me, as I forgave him or her.

I put gusto into the Inventory, motivated by my desire to feel the depth of the love emotion. It took nearly three hours to complete, and I was exhausted but lighthearted when it was over. Afterward, my heart felt like it had been dusted off and was now a cleaner conduit of emotion.

Listening for Guidance

My dealings with the angels (and unknowingly, with the fairies) were so illuminating that I joyously asked for and awaited their suggestions. So, the following morning, I eagerly placed my notebook and pen in my hip pack and headed for the beach. *What will I learn today?* I wondered as I greeted the bougainvillea along Selva Avenue, and unabashedly buried my face in its bright purple blossoms.

With exuberance, I bounded down the Dana Strands Beach staircase. Midway down the stairs, I stopped to admire the tropical-looking cove with its gorgeous palm trees and clear turquoise water. Not only was the view magnificent, but so was the fragrance of wild tuber roses and salty sea air. *Thank you, angels, for getting me out of the house so that I can discover the rich beauty of Mother Nature,* I mentally said, my heart filled with gratitude.

"Head to the left," the angels instructed me through an

inner voice and emotional feelings that acted like a dowsing rod. Obediently, I strode along the sand toward a large boulder. *"Sit there,"* the angels advised, indicating a granite rock. I noticed that it was smoothly eroded, with an indentation large enough to sit upon, like a natural saddle chair.

I settled onto the granite throne and closed my eyes to meditate. *What would you like me to know?* I inwardly asked the angels.

"We'd like you to feel. Breathe deeply and just feel." I took several deep breaths, as my mind excitedly wondered what the angels would tell me.

"Just feel," they said. *"Don't try to second-guess or control what you will feel. To do so is to use your ego-mind. Just feel."*

The angels didn't want me to help the experience along by anticipating it. Anticipation would take me out of the present moment, causing me to focus on the future. *Just feel,* I instructed my mind, breathing deeply. *Just feel.* I focused on the sound of my breath, and the feeling the air created as I held it in different increments and intervals. I felt and heard my heartbeat slow down, and my head leaned forward with heaviness and blessed relaxation.

My back, bottom, legs, and hands rested comfortably on the warm granite. Its smooth surface reached up to touch me, supporting me gently yet firmly. I focused on breathing, feeling, breathing, feeling—until my breath synchronized with the crashing surf's rhythms. Each exhalation matched the sound of water pounding on the sand, and each inhalation echoed the sound of the surf retreating to the ocean.

The granite, too, seemed to breathe in sync with me and the surf. I felt the rock as a living, breathing entity. The sand granules seemed to sing a chorus in tune with the tenor of the seagulls. The palm trees rustled like a percussion section, as my heart softly acted as their metronome.

Without taking myself out of the moment, I realized with pleasure and astonishment: *Oh, my gosh! Everything is alive!* I grasped that every bit of matter has a life force, gathered from the Creator's life-infusing energy. I felt one with the surf, the sand, the sun, the seagulls, and the granite rock.

As I focused on the rock's life force, I understood that Earth represented an even greater reflection of this living being. It breathed, it felt emotions, it grew, and it evolved. I knew that I (along with every other soul) was part of this living Earth.

"*Yes,*" the angels whispered to me, "*it is true that every single thing is alive. The rock is composed of granite and quartz crystal, and it is what you refer to as an 'elemental' being. It is related to the fairies and the other elemental beings you will soon call your 'friends.'*

"*The rocks and the crystals are absorbers and amplifiers,*" they went on, explaining that granite has absorbed wisdom from the Universal Mind, or collective unconscious. It was a library of sorts, filled with important spiritual wisdom and messages. The rocks and crystals also augmented the loudness and clarity of any spiritual insights I might receive while in their vicinity, as well as amplifying my prayers and conversations with heaven.

So, anytime I wanted help hearing God, the angels, the fairies, or anyone in the spirit world, I could sit upon a rock formation and be connected to a spiritual megaphone. I could hear and be heard, louder and clearer, with the help of granite, crystals, and other members of the mineral family.

❧ ❧ ❧

CHAPTER 3

Connecting with the Fairies

When I left the beach, I walked slowly up the staircase. The angels had taught me the value of literally stopping and smelling the roses. I pulled the wild tuber roses to my nose and deeply inhaled their perfumey fragrance. It was a sweet scent reminiscent of exotic honey.

I had started to clairvoyantly see fairies flying around flowers, and I wondered if I could hear them, too. Up until now, it seemed that all of my information about fairies had just come from the angels.

So, I walked along a desolate dirt path that connected Dana Strand Drive, past the park, to Selva Drive.

The shrubs waved in the wind at me, and I mentally called to them, *Hello! If anyone in there can hear me, please speak to me!* I knew that fairies were shy beings and that they ran away from anyone who possessed harsh energy or manipulative intentions, so I carefully monitored my heart's energy, making sure that I was speaking to them from love and not from fear.

Hello, fairies, leprechauns, and anyone from the elemental kingdom! I mentally called out. I realized that beings from heaven could hear our thoughts, so I didn't need to voice my communications aloud. I'd never had any difficulty making verbal contact with God, the Holy Spirit, angels, deceased people, animals, or ascended masters through this style of mental communication.

However, for some reason, I doubted whether the fairies could actually hear me and whether I would hear them. Maybe it was because I felt that the fairies had *conditional* love for us humans, while the angels and other spiritual beings were *unconditionally* loving. Whatever the reason, for the first time I doubted whether I could make the spiritual connection successfully. *This helps me to better understand my workshop members who have doubts about their telepathic abilities,* I thought. *So this is a blessing that I'm having doubts.*

Yet I could clearly see the fairies by this time. I saw them, partly in my mind's eye, and partly with my physical eyes (much like I see other heavenly beings). I could see fairies flitting about flowers and plants, and water "sprite" fairies dancing around the surf and tide pools.

The fairies were about one inch high—very thin females dressed in short white dresses with handkerchief hemlines. I couldn't distinguish many individual traits when comparing one fairy to the other; most of them had a uniform appearance, although I'd occasionally see fairies who exuded a pink or light green color, rather than a white glow.

They looked like fireflies in movement—being here, there, here, there—in a sort of beelike race among the flowers and leaves. They seemed like miniature nurses, conducting hospital rounds to check on the patients (the foliage). Their movements were so quick that I couldn't see their wings flap. Rather, they blurred like hummingbirds in flight.

The fairies' diminutive size definitely distinguished them from the angels, who ranged from one to ten feet in height. In addition, angels' wings had feathers and were bird-like, whereas fairies had wings like butterflies or dragonflies.

Interestingly, angels never used their wings for transportation. The angels explained that they only appeared with wings so that we would recognize them. Apparently, the early Renaissance painters mistook the angels' aura glow for wings, so they painted them that way. Ever since, the angels have shape-shifted to meet our expectations. Angels transport themselves—not through wing-propelled flight, but through mental manifestation. In other words, they imagine where they want to be, and they're instantly there.

Fairies, in contrast, *do* use their wings to get around. Even though they're much smaller than angels, fairies have denser bodies—similar to the difference between the weight of a large cloud versus a wooden pencil. So, while the fairies are brilliant manifesters, they still rely upon the physics of wings to transport themselves.

"Sprites," or water fairies, don't have wings. These beings, who are the protectors of water bodies, are about three inches tall and one-half inch across. They are rather shapeless and often appear as nude, opalescent bodies of light. Just as the fairies are the guardian angels of land mammals, so are sprites the guardian angels of water birds and seafowl.

Fairy Guides, Spirit Guides

Frequently I'd see fairies around human beings, acting like guardian angels. Often, these were individuals with a Celtic heritage. So, I wondered, did Welsh, Scottish, or Irish people (my own ancestry) attract fairies who acted alongside our guardian angels?

During my spiritual counseling sessions, I saw a consistent pattern among my clients: People whose guardians were fairies usually had a life purpose involved with helping plants, animals, or the environment. These individuals' constitutions could not withstand working indoors, especially in office cubicles. Their souls needed to work outdoors, or at least they needed to have careers involving an environmental cause. They made wonderful plant nursery employees, animal sitters, veterinarians, forestry workers, public aquarium docents, and oceanographers.

Yet, even though I could see the fairies, when it came to hearing and talking with them, I was unclear and unsure. I felt as if I were shouting down a dark tunnel when I spoke to them, and I wondered if they could actually hear me. Maybe I'd be relegated to only seeing, and not hearing, the fairies!

Learning More about the Fairies

Every afternoon and evening when I sat at my computer, I'd pray for protection and assistance, and then I'd feel myself go into a trance. I'd lose consciousness of my surroundings and would only vaguely be aware of my hands typing the text of *Angel Therapy*. I really didn't know the gist of what I was typing, and I never read the material when the typing ceased. Afraid that I'd be confronted with pages full of gibberish, I told myself that I'd read the book when it was completed.

The first half of the book consisted of short chapters channeled by the angels on topics such as "Depression," "Anger," and "Dating." The angels dictated the chapters, but they weren't given to me in any particular order—alphabetical or otherwise. The last chapter that they dictated was one titled "Child Abuse." The angels then indicated that, with their help, I would write the second half of the book, which would serve as a guide to working with the angels.

I still wasn't ready to read the channeled chapters, though, so I immediately began working on the second half of *Angel Therapy*. The final chapters were dictated to me as practical, how-to messages about how to get in touch with our angels. I was aware of this information as it came to me, because its down-to-earth material allowed me to be in a more aware state. One chapter that the angels "wrote" was about "nature angels," or the fairies.

As I mentioned in the Preface, I learned the necessity of warning the fairies before walking on the grass, picking flowers, and mowing the lawn. They said that the warning was a courtesy to the fairies so they wouldn't be harmed or frightened. Although they had spiritual bodies, material objects could still affect the density of their bodies. Warning the fairies was our duty if we wanted to treat them with love and respect, and something that could be conveyed mentally or aloud to them. Well, that made perfect sense to me. I'd already ascertained the importance of warning fairies before mowing the lawn, but it hadn't occurred to me that our feet could harm them, too. So, I began putting this advice into practice. During the next day's walk, I tried to avoid walking on the park lawn when going to the beach, choosing the sidewalks instead.

When I got home, the garage door was open, and my husband, Michael, was pushing the electric lawnmower toward the backyard. Although I knew he wouldn't believe me, I adamantly told him that I needed to warn the fairies before he began mowing. He said, "Fine," like someone who had long ago realized the futility of arguing with me about such matters.

I stepped onto the back patio and mentally called to the fairies: *My husband will be here in a moment with a sharp and noisy lawnmower. Please scurry away so you don't get hurt or frightened.* Within a moment, the lawn was eerily quiet, as if all life had left the area.

I called to Michael to tell him that the coast was clear. While I could see that he didn't believe me, at least he didn't argue. He mowed the lawn while I got busy in my home office.

I waited until that afternoon to go on my walk. I strapped on my hip pack, complete with the little notebook and pen I kept by my side to capture the angels' wisdom. *"Take two plastic bags,"* I heard the voice firmly guide me, and so I pushed two plastic shopping bags into the hip pack.

Plant Spirits

As I walked past the shrubbery near the beach, I could see green, leaf-covered friendly faces staring at me. I intuitively knew that these were "plant spirits" or "bush people," relatives of the fairies, and part of the elemental kingdom. I mentally greeted the nature spirits. In my mind's ear, I could hear their distinctly male voices reply, *"And how are you today?"* I stopped. Was that my imagination? A product of wishful thinking?

"How are you today?" the voices chimed in unison again. Obviously, they expected an answer. I mentally replied, *I'm fine, thank you.*

"Good, you seemed a little rushed yesterday." I was amazed by the casual nature of our conversation. Unlike the etheric energy and content of my dealings with the angels, this felt more like talking with a next-door neighbor. It also felt strangely familiar, as if I'd spoken with these nature spirits before.

"Say, would you be a love and pick those up?" I felt my gaze turn toward some fast-food containers that were strewn on the ground. I hesitated momentarily, thinking that they looked awfully sticky with their dried catsup and syrupy cola. Then I overcame my self-consciousness and pulled the plastic bags from my hip pack. As I placed the trash inside, I wondered if the nature spirits were the ones who'd told me to bring the bags.

As I continued my walk, I felt strongly compelled to pick up more litter along the way. *"Sorry, but we can't do it ourselves,"* I heard the nature spirits say. *"We need you humans to help us take care of planet Earth by salvaging and recycling these bits of trash."* I was told to not only pick up the trash along my walk, but to make sure that paper, aluminum, and glass were recycled! Fortunately, Dana Point had an extensive recycling program. Each house received two trash cans, one for recyclables, and one for nonrecyclables.

The next day, I brought an even larger trash bag with me on my walk. As I sauntered along the sand, I placed the discarded candy wrappers, plastic six-pack carriers, and other trash into my bag. *What were these people thinking when they threw their litter on the sand?* I angrily thought as I picked up each bit of garbage. *Don't they know that this trash could kill seagulls if they swallowed it?*

Annoyed by the carelessness of each litterbug, I felt myself growing more tense with each step I took. I'd never noticed how much refuse was strewn on the sand until the nature spirits had requested my help in cleaning it up.

"Being angry with them won't help to heal the situation," I heard as I stooped to pick up yet another empty potato chip bag. *"The people who were careless with their litter need your energy of love so that they'll grow spiritually. This will increase their sensitivity to the environment so they will know the impact of their actions upon other living creatures."*

Of course! I should send the litterers love, not only for their own growth, but also so that I wouldn't be swallowed by resentment. I suddenly felt sorry for whoever had discarded the potato chip bag in my hand. To have performed such a thoughtless deed, the individual must have minimal awareness about the interconnectedness of life to the planet.

"Whoops—judging them is another form of attack!" I heard the voice counsel me. I wasn't sure who was talking to me initially—it sounded wise and esoteric, like the angels, yet I'd never heard an angel say "Whoops" before. I figured that I must be hearing the elementals!

I mentally asked, *Are you the bush people or the fairies?*

I felt a strong presence above my right shoulder and knew that this was the direction where the voice came from. *"Yes, it's true. Some of your guardian angels are fairies. Please don't be afraid. We are beings of Divine essence and light. If you'll sit down, we'll show you."*

Healing with the Fairies

My breath deepened as I obediently sat on the sand. *"We'd like to show you our healing abilities. You may want to lie down to experience this,"* they told me through a wordless inner voice, which was more like thought transference than the spoken voices I'd heard from the angels.

I unzipped my sweatshirt and put it on the sand to rest my head upon. I lay down on my back, looking at the thin cloud over the beach. Suddenly I felt glued to the sand, and I had a mental image of Gulliver covered with Lilliputians and ropes.

"Don't be afraid," they repeated. *"We are working on your energy field, what you call your 'aura.'"* The fairies explained that they were cleaning the negative energy that was stuck around my body. Like fish that suction barnacles off of sea creatures, I felt the fairies cleaning me. It was over within minutes, and I could move my arms and legs once again.

As I stood up, a cloud parted, revealing a blue sky and sunshine. My body reflected this vision, feeling youthful. It was similar to the sensation that I've had after a chiropractic adjustment or a massage, where I've felt greater freedom of movement even though I hadn't noticed how tense I'd been before.

I realized that the fairies worked on us whenever we went outside in nature, or were in close proximity to animals or plants. So that was why I always felt refreshed after my beach walks. It wasn't just the exuberance brought about by physical exercise and the sea breezes—it was the fairies clearing the air around me that created the fresh air in my aura!

🌸 🌸 🌸

CHAPTER 4

Signs from the Fairies

It rained that night—hard. When I went downstairs to ensure that the bedroom windows were shut, I was horrified to see that the sliding glass door was wide open. Michael had come through the door earlier in the evening, and he'd apparently forgotten to close it behind him.

"Romeo!" I frantically shouted. My Himalayan cat, declawed and oh-so-trusting, was a pure housecat. Since we lived near busy Golden Lantern Boulevard, we kept him inside to avoid the 40-mile-an-hour traffic, the coyotes known to frequent the area, and neighborhood dogs. Romeo didn't seem to fear vehicles or other animals, and if he got outside, his naiveté would put him in danger.

"Michael, is Romeo with you?" I hollered up the staircase.

"I'll look," he said with concern. A few moments later, he yelled down to me, "I can't find him up here."

I grabbed a flashlight and headed out into the stormy night. "Romeo!" I called. "Romeo, where are you?" Everything looked black and wet—the lawn, the bushes, the sidewalk. Romeo was probably wet and frightened, hiding someplace. How would I ever find him?!

"Pray," the thought came to me. Of course! Just as I could talk to the angels about any individuals with whom I was having trouble, so too could I talk to my cat's guardian angels! I held the intention to speak with Romeo's angels, which I now knew to be fairies, as they are for all animals and birds.

Mentally, I spoke to Romeo's fairies. *Please help me. Please tell Romeo to come home, or come to me when I call him. Please lead me to him.* For good measure, I also appealed to the Archangels Michael and Raphael. The former helps us to feel courageous in times of fear, and the latter helps to heal our bodies. *It can't hurt to call in the big guns,* I thought. I appealed to everyone I could think of to help find my cat.

Moments later, my flashlight reflected two round objects, and I knew I was looking at Romeo's big eyes. There he was, out past our driveway, looking as if he'd just climbed out from under the thick shrubbery. He crouched and allowed me to pick him up.

So, was it the archangels, the saints, or the fairies who helped me rescue my cat? I believe they worked together as a team, handling the minor and major details of guiding Romeo and me so that we'd meet at the perfect moment.

Natural Beauty

I was grateful for the fairies' assistance and friendship. I would hear from them on a daily basis, especially when I walked near the wildflowers and brush. *"We prefer natural settings,"* they told me, *"and are more apt to be in a wild growth area, rather than an artificially manicured garden."*

Their words reminded me of the beautiful overgrown yards I'd seen in southern England years earlier. There, gardens are overrun with gorgeous flowers and viney plants. The yards lacked any visible weeds or dried leaves, similar to a beautiful young woman with a perfect complexion wearing little makeup and a casual hairstyle. Like the fairies, I preferred the wild look to the tightly controlled, typical American garden.

The sunshine returned to Orange County two days following Romeo's disappearance. Rain never stayed for long in Southern California, like the saying goes. The terrain was washed clean as I admired the sparkling leaves on the bougainvillea. Fortunately, the heavy rain hadn't beaten the flowers away. As they reached toward the sun, they seemed more vividly purple than ever.

I finished my walk by going into the backyard. *Hmm, I better tell Michael about this,* I thought, as I noticed a big patch of toadstools that had suddenly appeared full-grown by the slumpstone wall. Michael, the tender of the yard, would undoubtedly have an opinion on what to do.

"I took care of them," he told me later. Michael explained that he'd cut them down. "I just can't figure out how the mushrooms got so big so quickly," he said. "They weren't there when I mowed the lawn three days ago."

The next morning, I took my time getting out of bed. I lay there awhile, looking at the backyard out the window and sliding glass door. I gasped at the sight of dozens of dew-decorated flowers that had blossomed everywhere—orange lilies, garlic flowers bursting with purple, sunshiny marigolds, and the same wild tuber roses that I saw on my beach walks. *How had they bloomed so rapidly?* I wondered.

I put on my robe and slippers and opened the sliding glass door to get a better look. I saw fairy families tending to the tuber roses, holding what looked like buckets, in which they gathered and distributed something that apparently created rapid growth. I noted, however, that there wasn't the abundance of fairy folk here, as compared to those near the wild plants on the beach walk.

The foliage was thick, except for one open patch between the garden and the patio. An angel statue would look beautiful there, I decided. I only had a few angel statues, and none of them were suitable for outdoor use. Oh, there was the beautiful concrete birdbath I'd received as a Christmas present. A foot-high cherub sat atop a large alabaster shell that held water for the birds who delighted in splashing and bathing themselves. But it wasn't the statue I visualized in the little clearing by the garden.

Feed the birds, I thought. But did I really initiate that thought, or did someone whisper it into my ear? *Feed the birds,* I heard again. Since the guidance fit in with my natural tendencies, I didn't question it. So that afternoon, I bought a bucket of high-quality wild birdseed at the pet store.

As is my tendency, I went a little overboard in feeding the birds. Was I making up for lost time, enthusiastically following my guidance, or just engaging in a pleasurable pursuit? Whatever the case, I filled two large bowls with birdseed and placed them on the patio near the clearing.

Then, for good measure, I poured a three-inch-thick line of seed along the top of the slumpstone wall and sat back to wait for customers. Like any goal that is too forcefully intended, mine took awhile to manifest. It wasn't until the early afternoon, when I'd gotten distracted with my work, that I noticed three sparrows perched on the wall, busily pecking at the seed. Although they might have just been "ordinary" sparrows, I was transfixed by their natural beauty and movement.

The following morning, I awoke to the sound of, "Crrroooo, crrrooooo." Remembering my new bird friends, I leaped out of bed and almost startled the three mourning doves eating out of the patio bowls. "Look, look!" I excitedly ran into Grant's bedroom and pointed at the birds visible outside his window.

"Oh, wow," my son said, obviously appreciative, but lacking the near-fanatical passion I was displaying. Hypnotized as I was by the mourning doves' angelic coos and countenance, two hours slipped by unawares.

When I returned home from my afternoon beach walk, I noticed that a small package was sitting on my porch. The return address told me that my mother had shipped a birthday gift to me, several days early. *Should I wait to open it?* I wondered. Something told me to indulge in the gift immediately.

As I opened the box and pulled out the carefully wrapped contents, I wondered what my mother had bought. So wrapped up in my newfound fairy friends, as well as completing the final pages of *Angel Therapy*, I hadn't talked to my mom for at least three weeks. She had no idea of my current adventures and interests, and I vowed to call and thank her for the gift later that day.

As I removed the paper, my eyes caught the sight of terra cotta clay. It was a statue! How did she know? Expecting an angel that I could put into the clearing, I was thrilled and surprised to unwrap a beautiful outdoor statue of a fairy! Now I wondered more than ever how my mother had been so prescient. We'd never spoken of my new attraction to fairies, and she'd never mentioned her interest in them either.

Yet, my mother, one of the most spiritually minded people I'd ever known, was at the center of so many of my life's miracles and mystical experiences. Why should I question the fact that her gift supported my current pursuits?

As I carefully placed the adobe fairy in the clearing, my heart warmed as I thought about how rapidly my vision of the statue had manifested. Far from being idols of worship— after all, the angels had adamantly taught me to give all glory to God and not to worship or pray to them—the statues seemed like symbols of God's love. They were gentle reminders to look heavenward when life became stressful. I'd also discovered that people who kept angel statues tended to have more guardian angels around them and in their homes. Could the same hold true for fairies? After all, fairies had proven to be powerful friends and healers for me. Maybe keeping a fairy statue in the yard would be like unleashing bees or ladybugs—friendly helpers of the garden.

I positioned the statue until it was at just the right angle to suit me—so that I could see the fairy from my bed. I stepped back to admire it when something to my right caught my eye. As I walked toward some light-colored objects, I was shocked to discover that the toadstools had returned, but this time, they looked more abundant and robust than ever!

That evening, I told Michael about the mushrooms in the yard. He immediately went out there with a shovel to dig them up. I heard him mutter something about the bizarre nature of their sudden full-grown reappearance.

Messages from Heaven

I went into my home office to work on *Angel Therapy,* and after closing the door and turning on the dimly colored lights, I said a prayer for guidance. I only had a few more chapters to go, according to the angels. I still hadn't attempted to read the book's first half of channeled angel messages. I'd promised myself that upon the book's completion, I'd start reading them.

However, I realized that I was procrastinating delving into what might turn out to be a painful process. What if the messages were unintelligible? I had no idea how I'd handle such an unthinkable situation. Already, I'd put months into the writings, and my publisher's deadline was rapidly approaching. The book had been presold to chain and metaphysical stores, and they expected it by a certain date.

As I sat in front of the computer, I gazed at the beautiful poster in front of me—it was a painting whose likeness would grace the cover of *Angel Therapy:* "L'Innocence" by William Bouguereau. I looked at the beautiful brunette's beatific expression as she cupped her ears to better hear the cherub's messages. *Maybe I should cup my ears so that I can focus on completing the book,* I mused. I got up from my chair and lay down on the office floor, but something was too artificial, too unnatural about the setting, so I grabbed two large bath towels and headed toward the patio.

It was a gorgeous evening with a brilliant full moon. I put the towels on my patio's chaise lounge and lay down. I'd never before been on the chaise lounge after sunset. Now it felt like I was taking a "moon bath." Ice-blue light poured over me, awakening some ancient feminine stirrings from deep within my soul.

I opened my arms wide to gather more moonlight. It

seemed that I was hungrily drinking in its energy. In the distance, I could see the moon shimmering reflectively on the ocean that met the Dana Point Harbor. The moonlight and I communed for a timeless hour or two.

The next morning's colors seemed brighter. Maybe the moon bath had washed away some psychic dirt from my physical and spiritual sight!

The backyard garden buzzed with life: vibrant flowers, huge leaves, joyful birds, and the ever-hungry squirrels. Baby birds and squirrels were introduced by their parents to the banquet that I laid out for them each day. One fat little baby bird, whose girth seemed broader than that of his mother, cheeped incessantly until she put chewed-up birdseed into his beak. He'd follow her every move, constantly begging for more food.

I realized that my backyard's new growth and inhabitants were evidence of the fairies' presence. I had an insight that must have come from the fairy realm, due to its strength and completeness: *"Those who don't yet see fairies can instead see proof of their reality. Look for the blooming flowers, taller plants, butterflies, dragonflies, birds, and squirrels. You are seeing the fairies' invited guests in your backyard visitor's presence. You are witnessing the fairies' signature artwork in your garden's increased growth. The fairies only ask that you take good care of the soil, plants, birds, and animals in return."*

So the fairies were pleased by my recent spurt of garden caretaking and bird tending! It was true that I'd adopted a new habit of spending time in the garden, watering and planting. And I delighted in making sure that the birds and squirrels were well fed. The number of golden-gray mourning doves visiting my various bird feeders had risen dramatically, and I now counted 20 of them at a time.

Even my eating habits reflected my love of birds and

animals. The angels had adjusted my diet several years earlier, in response to my prayers to become more clairvoyant and intuitive.

"You are eating the energy of pain every time you ingest animal flesh," they'd explained. *"The animal's suffering creates chemicals that flow through its flesh, and when you eat that animal, you are ingesting pain. Pain lowers your frequency and prevents you from hearing messages from the high planes of the spirit world. If you really want to be able to see and hear across the veil, stop eating meat. Dairy products are clogging your aura as well, and your 'window screen' into heaven will be clearer if you avoid dairy."*

After receiving this message, I had stopped eating animal products, including dairy items. I continued to eat fish, however, as the angels explained that a fish's watery environment transmuted the energy of their pain. However, one evening when I was cooking swordfish for my family, I noticed the blood from the filet pooling in the frying pan. *That's blood from a being that was once alive,* I thought to myself, horrified at the realization. I immediately gave up eating fish. I was fortunate in that my new vegan diet completely satisfied me, and also helped me feel very energetic and healthful. I didn't crave meat, poultry, fish, or dairy products at all.

In a related note, it's interesting to point out that at my "Connecting with Your Angels" workshops, I had been successful in teaching audience members how to receive messages from their angels. In one exercise, students are paired with a stranger and taught to give an "angel reading" (similar to a psychic reading, except you intentionally get information from the other person's guardian angels, instead of allowing messages from random members of the spirit world to come through). During the exercise, I would instruct participants to ask their partner's angels the following questions: "How can my partner be better able to see and hear you? Are there any changes that my partner can make that will enable her to better see and hear you?"

I was amazed by the number of people who heard a response that said, essentially, *"Tell her to cut down on how much cheese (or ice cream, butter, etc.) she eats."* I found that I could actually see evidence of high dairy-product consumption in someone's aura: It looked and felt filmy, like a window with grease smeared on it.

One time I told Carolyn, a spiritual counseling student of mine, that her aura showed an extremely high dairy content. She was amazed that her recent milk-product binges were visible and palpable in her energy field. When I saw Carolyn one month later, she looked wonderful! She explained that she'd given up all dairy products after asking her angels to heal her cravings—and she'd dropped ten pounds!

I realized that the fairies were also involved in suggesting these dietary changes, yet their motivations differed from that of the angels. Whereas the angels were simply answering my prayers for better spiritual connections, the fairies knew that veganism was a more Earth-friendly lifestyle. Over the next few days, they explained that organic farming was essential to reviving the soil's life force, which had deadened in response to pesticide-based farming. They also urged me to educate myself about animal rights.

This was easy for me to do, because two nights earlier, I'd had a haunting dream: A herd of rhinoceroses galloped along the Serengeti Plain, and one rhino looked right at me. I plainly heard his voice appeal to me, *"Help us! Please help us!"* I felt the pain and fear of the rhinos, and woke up with hot tears of grief clinging to my eyes. Yet I didn't know how to help these beautiful creatures who lived on a faraway continent.

So the fairies' encouragement to research the plight of animals spurred me to try to respond to the rhinos' request. This made sense to me, as I'd learned that the fairies' main purpose is to protect plants and animals. Yes, they are friends and helpers to humankind, too; however, their primary concern is for the voiceless two- and four-legged inhabitants of Mother Earth.

I went on the Internet and searched for information on animal protection groups, finding two that particularly appealed to me: People for the Ethical Treatment of Animals (PETA) and EarthSave (more information about these groups can be found at the back of this book). I started to volunteer on behalf of PETA, advocating kindness to animals.

Through my research, I was shocked to discover just how cruelly animals are treated when they are raised for leather and food. The birds and animals are kept in tiny cages, with no room to turn around. They exist in an absolute living hell. When I discovered that the cows used in leather products are also tortured and malnourished, I immediately swore off using any leather products. I donated all of my leather shoes and purses, replacing them with fashionable "microfiber" items. The fairies gave me big thumbs-up for making a difference, and for educating others, too.

Having become a staunch supporter of animal rights, you can imagine my surprise when I received a message from the souls of animals who had passed on one evening. Almost like a collective voice, they said to me, *"We don't mind you humans using us for food or clothing. It's the way that you treat us while you are raising us that's the problem."*

The message took my breath away, because up until that time, I believed that it was wrong—no matter how an animal was raised—to use it for food or clothing. But the fairies explained it this way: *"You can choose to use no animal products, and there is definite virtue in doing so. Yet, look at how much the animals love you humans. Look at how devoted they are to your external happiness that they would give their own lives for you. They must be suffering greatly to even complain about their mal-treatment. Help them, please. Be a voice for them, please. Create awareness of their suffering and pain, and we will do all we can to help you in this endeavor, now and always."*

❧ ❧ ❧

CHAPTER 5

Visions and Dreams

I was seeing fairies all the time, especially among the flowers. The fairies explained how some of them are "assigned" to certain ones. If those flowers are cut into a bouquet, several fairies will stay with it until the life force leaves the flower. It's similar to the way a guardian angel will stay with a human until their last dying breath, and then accompany that soul on its journey home to heaven.

I was amazed that I hadn't noticed the fairies until I reached my adult years. Looking back at my childhood, I clearly remember seeing deceased people and the evidence of guardian angels. I recalled when my family moved (when I was two years old) to our home on Craner Avenue in North Hollywood (in L.A.'s San Fernando Valley). It was there that I had my first "mediumistic" experiences—although I didn't know it at the time.

All I knew was that I *saw* people—opaque and very alive-looking—whom others didn't see. One evening, for instance, I called my mother into my bedroom and told her that "the people" kept staring at me. I could see adults, but I didn't recognize them as deceased relatives. They were complete strangers, and I could see them as clearly as I could see my mother. She didn't see anything, though, and told me that since she and my father had been in the living room watching television, the people I was seeing must have been images from the TV set reflected in my bedroom window. But that didn't make any sense at all. People on television moved and spoke. These people just stood there and stared.

I had some very deep friendships with the other children on Craner Avenue. David, Jody, Colleen, and I played together daily. I also spent a lot of time with my best friend, Stephanie, whose parents managed the apartment building at the end of our cul-de-sac. Her upstairs neighbor, Steven, was one of the cutest boys I'd ever seen. From age five onward, I had a hopeless crush on him, but he never seemed to notice me, since I was ten years younger. So, I was relegated to staring at Steven from afar, telling Stephanie how I wished that he would notice me.

Steven and I only interacted a few times. One time, he held an impromptu neighborhood show in which he demonstrated his ventriloquism talents with his Jerry Mahoney doll. I sat transfixed in the audience of kids in a neighbor's garage, watching Steven talk to the doll. Afterward, I asked him endless questions about the mechanisms of throwing one's voice, and how the doll's mouth and eyes moved. I admired him so much—my first crush!

Another time, my friends and I were playing a ball game on David's front lawn. I looked over and saw a man crouched in the bushes, watching us. I mentioned this to my friends, and they glanced at the bushes. "There's no one there, Doreen!" they insisted.

The kids at school were less than kind with their retorts when I'd talk about metaphysical concepts or my visions. I was beginning to understand that I was seeing people who were not visible to others. I also realized that my thoughts about life differed from others, too, so I became more cautious in reporting what I saw and thought.

My childhood visions were unnerving at times—mostly because I didn't understand them—yet they were never gory or Halloween-like, and I always felt safe. I felt especially secure and loved when they would come to my bedroom at night. I didn't see them as figures at first; I saw their glowing, twinkling "angel lights" instead. Sparkling shades of green, blue, and purple danced around me. With the lights came a deep sense of peace and an unearthly silence, as if I had fallen into a black hole where worldly sounds didn't exist.

With age, my clairvoyance shifted. I saw deceased people less opaquely, and more as translucent, three-dimensional characters who appeared in my mind's eye and my physical vision simultaneously. Like the holographic ballroom dancers in the Disneyland ride "The Haunted Mansion," deceased people looked decidedly different from living people.

My angel visions, on the other hand, became more *detailed* as I grew older. I could see angels' faces, bodies, and wings, in addition to their glowing lights. In the same way that I saw deceased people, I simultaneously saw the angels with inner and outer vision.

I still didn't talk about my visions, for fear of ridicule. I only shared the information that the spirit world imparted to me, without saying where or how I received the knowledge. Even then, I "cleaned up" their messages before sharing them with other people so that the words would sound mainstream.

As I grew up, got married, had my two sons, and went to college, I was still in contact with the spirit world, although the angels actually seemed to be more like pests, than friends, to me. They constantly urged me to speak and write about the metaphysical truths they'd taught me, but my painful childhood memories of being teased still stung. When I became established as a psychotherapist and author in the eating-disorder field, I feared that if I spoke openly about my spirit world dealings, I would lose my reputation, income, and friends. In the late 1980s and early '90s, as a divorced mother of two, I focused less on spirituality and more on making enough money to survive.

In 1993, I felt that I was ready to remarry, so I focused my intentions on using the principles of manifestation to meet my future husband. First, I wrote a detailed list of everything I desired in a mate, only writing about the characteristics that truly mattered to me in a bluntly self-honest fashion. Once the list was complete, I emotionally gave it to God. I mentally affirmed, *I know that this man is looking for me with the same fervor with which I'm looking for him.*

Within three weeks, I met Michael. He was everything that I had asked for on my list. I clearly understood that I had manifested him into my life through my positive intentions and my spiritual surrender. We became inseparable immediately, and we were engaged within one year. We seemed completely compatible—until a life-changing situation created monumental changes in my personal and professional life. Those changes would prove fatal to our marriage.

Back on the Spiritual Path

It happened on July 15, 1995, when a male angel loudly and clearly warned me that my car was going to be stolen. One hour later, two armed men demanded my car keys and purse and jumped me. The angel told me to resist, to scream with all my might. My shrieks attracted the attention of some bystanders, who frightened the men away.

I was never the same after that day. I began researching Divine interventions, taking psychic development courses, praying, meditating, and consuming metaphysical books. However, I felt that every time I discussed my new interests with Michael, he was skeptical and patronizing. It reminded me of the reactions my school friends had when I'd mentioned metaphysics or psychic phenomena as a child. I pulled back from talking with my husband, and I felt us growing apart.

Why hadn't I put "spirituality"on my list when I'd been trying to manifest a mate? Well, at the time, it didn't seem like a high priority to me. Yet now, when I realized that I craved having a partner with whom to discuss consciousness and life-after-death, I mentally kicked myself for leaving such a crucial detail off my manifestation list. I loved Michael, but I felt a barrier between us. Intellectually, I knew that he was just as "spiritual" as I was. After all, we're all spirits. We're all children of God. *But I wish I could talk about these concepts with him,* I would pray.

Over the next few months, I asked Michael to accompany me to a *Course in Miracles* discussion group, and to Sunday-evening meetings at the local Religious Science church. He dutifully attended, yet afterward, I would feel angry when we'd talk about the workshops. It seemed to me that he wanted to debate, not discuss, so I stopped talking openly with him about my love of spirituality. Instead, I would talk with my close friends at the study groups and church. Unfortunately, as I pulled away from Michael, the energy in our relationship started to dissipate.

Trusting my Divine Guidance

I tried to not think about my marriage, which was easy since I had become very busy giving lectures and writing books. The angels had asked me to give up my traditional psychology practice and to stop writing mainstream self-help books and magazine articles. They urged me to bring my life into total authenticity by only engaging in activities that were meaningful to me. That meant focusing on my passion: spirituality.

However, the angels didn't tell me how I was going to make up the income that I'd lose by stopping my former lines of work. They simply asked me to walk in faith, assuring me that I'd be financially and emotionally fine if only I'd bring my life into integrity.

Practically the very day after I rid my schedule of every shred of mainstream work, I received a call from a woman named Deb Evans, the program director of the Whole Life Expo. "We'd like you to give a speech at our San Jose event about your book *'I'd Change My Life If I Had More Time.'*"

I was thrilled! Usually, speakers had to solicit the Whole Life Expo, and their chances of getting a time slot to even give an unpaid speech were very slim. Yet, in this case, the program director was calling *me*, offering me a paid speaking engagement when I hadn't even applied to be a speaker! I knew that heaven was keeping its promise to me. I was entering a new career as the spiritual teacher I was born to be.

After that, my speaking and writing career took off. I had nearly instantaneous validation from the Universe that I was finally on the right career path. Doors began opening virtually effortlessly. Everyone seemed to be happy with my work, including me. Eventually, I received so many speaking invitations that I had to hire a manager and staff to help me with scheduling.

However, all the travel involved with giving speeches around the country was taking a toll on my marriage, since Michael would only travel with me on occasion. At one point, he got into the business of selling clothing at my workshops, but bringing his merchandise with him made travel difficult and cumbersome. It got to the point where he stopped accompanying me to my long-distance events. On the road, many of the speakers would compare notes as to how to keep a marriage together and simultaneously maintain a career. "It isn't easy," I kept hearing. I knew that I was taking a huge risk in my personal life by stepping into the public speaking arena.

Yet, Divine guidance was so clearly telling me to give speeches that I had to trust that a higher plan was at work. I surrendered my attachment to the outcome about my marriage. Of course I didn't want to feel any pain, and I certainly didn't intend to cause Michael or anyone else pain either. But following the carjacking, my priority was to reach as many people as possible and let them know that angels and life-after-death really do exist.

I continued my beach walks, fitting them in around my travel schedule. *Angel Therapy* was now complete, and it was time for me to read the chapters that had been channeled. I was as nervous as the day I'd opened the Chapman University envelope telling me that I'd passed my comprehensive finals and gotten my master's degree. I didn't know whether I'd read unintelligible words or channeled wisdom.

It turned out I had nothing to worry about. Each chapter contained information that I'd never heard or read about previously, and used vocabulary that seemed almost foreign. A few times, I had to look up the angels' terminology in the dictionary, since I'd never even heard these words before. Aside from adding a few punctuation marks and correcting some minor spelling errors, the book was published verbatim. I learned a great deal from reading the book, and some parts, which I didn't understand, made perfect sense to me in the following years as my own experiences opened me up.

My editor, Jill Kramer, who had worked with me on several previous books, remarked that she *knew* that *Angel Therapy* was a channeled book. "Your writing style is so distinctive, Doreen," she said, "and the first half of this book doesn't sound anything like you!"

Dream Encounters

Around this same time, I started having a series of intense dream experiences. I was aware, upon awakening, that my spirit traveled somewhere during my sleep. I always vaguely remembered being in a classroom as a student. Sometimes I even performed some informal teaching duties, such as sitting around a boulder with a dozen other people and leading a philosophical discussion. Many mornings, I awoke exhausted from all the nocturnal learning and teaching.

The information imparted to me at night made perfect sense when I'd receive it during the dream, yet when I'd awaken, I couldn't remember a single parcel of information! On one of my beach walks, I asked my angels to explain this phenomenon.

They told me, *"You're traveling to the fourth dimension, where there are no time parallels. The information you are receiving only makes sense in a world that doesn't restrict its thinking to time and space limitations. So when you wake up in the third-dimensional world that focuses on clocks and calendars, the information doesn't make sense."*

I felt sad, because I remembered delighting in the information when I'd received it. I recalled saying to my spiritual teachers, "Yes, yes, of course. This makes perfect sense!" I wished so much that I could remember what they had taught me each night.

"Don't worry," the angels assured me. *"The information that you and the other humans learn each night becomes incorporated into your unconscious mind. The information is never lost, and it always benefits you, even if you cannot consciously remember it."*

When I returned home, I reread the angels' writings in *Angel Therapy* on the topic of time:

> *"Does the watch that is upon your wrist rule your anger? Does the position of its hands push you into thinking that you must rush along like the sweeping hand that chases the seconds? Is it not true that you expend great energy by keeping up with the incessant ticking of the time's keepers? And yet, do you not acknowledge that, though they be unstoppable, the human machine requires rest . . . ?*
>
> *"So we ask you to be in the light as you consider this competition with a time machine that you have foisted upon*

yourself. When we look among you and into your hearts, we do not find one single soul that agrees with this reckless competition of mind and machinery. You are meant to have breaths of delight, not mimic a timepiece as if it owns you. . . . Creation is born not of a pressure, but of a ceaseless joy that goes outward in celebration of its magnificence. Play, not work, is the heart of solution.

"For just one hour, pay no attention to the measurements that are on your wrist. Allow no thoughts of time to rest upon your mind or your lips. And watch the movement of your mind and being slow to a restfulness that gives birth to new ideas."

I gladly followed the angels' advice, and found that—as usual—they were correct. The less I looked at the clock or the calendar, the more freedom my mind seemed to have to notice original thoughts and ideas. I also felt freer and less pressured, and I vowed to never again return to the "time habit."

The next day at the beach, I sat on a quartz rock for my meditation. As I fingered the crystal pieces that jutted out of the rock, I closed my eyes and asked for guidance. I felt as if the rock itself was speaking directly to me, in concert with the fairies and angels that surrounded me. As the fairies had explained, the rock was amplifying the volume of the Divine messages. After all, quartz is used in radios and watches.

"Quantum physicists are currently experimenting with the issue of time," the angels and fairies suddenly said. I listened intently, realizing that they were explaining the answer to many of my questions about time. *"Within the next two decades, these scientists will have solid evidence that will change the way humans view time. The scientists will show that the human obsession with timepieces and calendars is limiting and restricting*

you. By constantly checking your watches and calendars, you are denying your ability to be in many places simultaneously—what you call bilocating, but in many more places than two."

Wow! I thought. *Now that makes sense. It's our belief in time and space restrictions that create the reality of those restrictions for ourselves.*

The fairies and angels continued to explain that, if we would just stop focusing on time and dates so much, we humans could regain our natural spiritual abilities to instantly manifest, teletransport, and conduct other feats that now seem *super*natural. They said that in the not-too-distant future, human beings will stop wearing watches and will rely on inner intuitive clocks instead.

When I returned home from the beach, I took off the watch that I'd always worn, deciding to only wear it during workshops or when it seemed really important to know the time. Also, at the suggestion of the angels, I made the commitment to set aside at least one day a week where I wouldn't schedule any appointments. The angels told me that it was important for people to take a break from clock-watching by enjoying a day off where we could free-form the day without needing to know what time it was. They assured me that all my responsibilities would be met on that day, but would be handled with less stress.

I woke up in the middle of that night's sleep, shocked to find myself awake and definitely not dreaming—floating on the ceiling! I could see my body below me on the bed next to Michael. We were both asleep, but I was out of my body! I panicked, wanting desperately to go back into my body but not knowing how. After all, I hadn't had an out-of-body experience, to my knowledge, since I was a child.

At that time, I was around eight years old and was walking out of Sunday School at the Unity Church of North

Hollywood. Suddenly I felt paralyzed, unable to move. The next thing I knew, I was staring at my body, *but I wasn't in it!* A man's voice (the same one that warned me of the carjacking) that emanated from above said, *"This is what you are here to teach, that which you are experiencing now, this separation of mind and body."* And then like a sudden breeze, I was back inside my body again.

But now, floating above my bed, getting back into my body didn't seem quite so easy. I had no idea how to reenter my self. Where were my guides and angels when I needed them? Then I heard several angels say to me in unison, *"Your sadness over your past is making our job difficult to work with you, in teaching and helping you."*

Okay, you have my attention. I'm listening, I thought.

Just then, I was vacuumed back into my body, like the smoke entering Jeannie's bottle in the old TV show. My mind reeled with shock. I lay awake but didn't want to try moving my body. I looked over at Michael, who was sound asleep. He hadn't noticed a thing. Dare I tell him what happened to me?

I felt the presence of great, large beings in the room, although I couldn't see them with my spiritual or physical eyes. They delivered information to me wordlessly, in a telepathic mind-transference: *"Your sadness over your children— over your divorce and custody arrangement—has filled your heart and mind with guilt. These feelings are blocking you from fully receiving our teachings, and from being the teacher you are meant to be."*

Their words instantly rang true, and I knew that I still did feel enormous guilt over my divorce from the boys' father a number of years ago. We had all suffered, as Larry and I had fought over custody of Chuck and Grant. He won the first court case; I won the second. The boys lost in many ways, and every time I saw any evidence of emotional scarring, I felt responsible.

Intellectually, I knew that the marriage would never have survived. Barely 20 years old when we married, we had two children by the time we were 22. We were stressed out by financial troubles and immaturity. All the odds were stacked against us, and our marriage collapsed after three and a half years. The guilt, however, had survived intact, as the angels pointed out that night.

I was a little dazed the next morning, wondering about the physics of being "out of my body," and about the angelic message regarding my sadness. Their words rang true as I walked to the beach. With each step, I became increasingly aware of heaviness in my heart. Not a stab-wound heaviness—more like a lingering weight tied around my chest, pulling me slightly down. The heaviness was just barely noticeable, so I hadn't thought to heal it, but the angels' message made me aware of its presence.

The beach was so foggy that I could barely see anything. Like walking inside a cloud, I breathed in the heavy mist and felt a sense of playful adventure as I walked along the sand. Pretty soon I found an appealing spot where I could sit down. Mentally, I appealed to the angels: *Okay, thank you for telling me that my sadness has interfered with my spiritual growth and mission. Now, can you help me with it?*

Apparently, that was all the permission that the angels needed! In reply, I heard an inner voice direct me to lie down on the sand. I removed my sweatshirt to form a beach blanket for my head, and rested flat on my back. *"Close your eyes and breathe deeply,"* I heard.

Within moments, I had a mental image of a scene from the book *Gulliver's Travels*. I could feel hundreds of tiny angels—the fairies!—covering my entire body. I felt paralyzed in a very peaceful sort of way, unable to move, and not *wanting* to move. I could feel the fairies working on me, almost like they were knitting or crocheting a blanket over me. As I tuned in, I understood what the fairies were actually doing. *Oh,* I realized, *they're cleaning the negativity out of my aura.* It was then that I saw them, in my mind's eye, picking the thought-forms of fear and sadness out of my body's energy field. They reminded me of a highly organized team of tiny fruit-pickers.

This process continued for nearly 20 minutes, as far as I could tell, since I didn't carry a watch. I also felt as if time stopped during the healing session. Then the paralysis lifted and I felt able to move my hands and fingers, then my arms. I tested my back by raising my head slightly, and found that my entire body once again followed my commands.

I stood up, slightly disoriented. The heavy fog still blanketed the beach, adding to the surreal sense of time and space. But any negativity was counterbalanced by my enormous welling-up of gratitude for the fairies' sweet attentiveness. In fact, I felt that my entire focus had shifted to one of thankfulness. *Maybe that was the healing!* I thought. Perhaps the fairies had helped me to truly know that everything in life was a blessing.

"Yes, it is," I heard the tiny voices say in unison. *"Everything that has happened to you has enabled you to grow, to be strong, and to strive. You need to see the blessing within each and every person and situation, like the bee sees the nectar deep within each flower. By focusing on these blessings, your inner Light shines away all the heaviness associated with each situation. This heaviness is what causes you humans to go into judgment and become depressed. So, cast away your cares and see your entire situation in the Light."*

I sat down again to process their words. So, what blessings

had my divorce and ensuing child-custody disputes brought about? Well, I could see that it certainly had made my children and me pull closer together. And just like the old Nietzsche phrase, "That which does not kill us makes us stronger," surviving the divorce had made me feel practically invincible. I knew that it had hurt my sons, but I could also see that they had become self-reliant and mature through the process.

In addition, the situation had sparked me to write my first book, *My Kids Don't Live with Me Anymore: Coping with the Custody Crisis*. Not only had that book—now out-of-print—helped the thousands of divorcing parents who had written me letters of gratitude, it had also catapulted my writing and speaking career.

Undoing the Effects of Errors

"You can perform an undoing on the situation." I received the message as an internal instruction, voiceless but commanding. I perked up, anxious to hear the messages that I was sure would follow. Sure enough, the fairies and angels told me to say mentally: *Some mistakes have been made in this situation. I ask that the effects of all mistakes be undone in all directions of time.* The affirmation reminded me of *A Course in Miracles*, and I wondered if its "author," Jesus, was now also speaking to me.

I didn't spend much time wondering, though, because I was too busy noticing the strong physical shuddering sensations in my body. I knew that this was from releasing negative emotions that were wedged and stored in my body's cells. I said the affirmation again to myself, while simultaneously focusing upon the topic of the divorce and ensuing custody battle: *Some mistakes have been made in this situation. I ask that the effects of all mistakes be undone in all directions of time.*

I kept repeating the affirmation until the shuddering stopped. Then my body was quiet, indicating that it had been cleared of the negative energy charges connected to the drama between my ex-husband and me. I sat there staring into the fog for a while. When I regained my energy level, I stood up and walked home.

I was now more peaceful and happy than when I'd gone to the beach that day, yet the fairies' work must have had an amnesia-like effect on me. It was as if I couldn't remember how sad I'd been. It seemed like I'd always felt this happy. I was glad that I didn't remember, because I didn't want to focus upon anything but positive thoughts and feelings. Besides, I knew in my heart that everything was going to be okay for everyone connected to that divorce: my two sons, my ex-husband, my former in-laws, my parents, and myself. The healing wasn't just for me—it was for everyone.

When I arrived home, I noticed that the garage door was open, and I could hear a large whirring sound coming from the backyard. Michael was mowing the lawn. The fairies! I bolted down the stairway and loudly asked him, "Did you warn the fairies?"

His expression conveyed the answer to me before he could stammer, "Um, no. I guess I forgot."

Is he patronizing me? I wondered. *Or is it his lack of experience with fairies and angels?*

I thought of the extensive healing I'd just undergone. Not wanting to undo its positive effects, I focused on Michael's positive qualities. I then mentally said to the fairies, *Forgive us! I'm sorry that Michael mowed the lawn without warning you first!*

I went into the house, and a few minutes later, Michael kissed me on the top of my head. "Man, those mushrooms in the corner of the lawn just keep coming back!" he said to me. "But I'm pretty sure I took care of them this time." I felt cold goose bumps, shuddering at the sound of his words. But I had no idea why.

Laguna Beach Dreams

The next morning, just before daybreak, I had another mystical dream experience. My beloved Grandma Pearl, who had passed away several years before, appeared to me. Her face was so vivid and her presence so intense that it seemed as if I were awake, visiting with her in person. As she spoke to me, I knew that this was no mere dream. Grandma Pearl really *was* with me.

She had come to me many times after her death, usually as a presence that I could sense standing next to me, or as a voice giving me guidance. She'd helped me to understand life-after-death like no one else, and I felt closer to her after her death than when she was alive.

In her dream-visitation, Grandma Pearl showed me a series of pictures. First, she revealed an oceanview home in Laguna Beach, California. Then, like a slide show, a new image flashed at me. This time I could see armless wooden chairs, upholstered in a maroon tapestry. I said to Grandma, "Oh! I remember those chairs!" I felt so happy to see them, feeling the sentimental memory and familiarity they evoked in my heart.

"Would you like this home and those chairs?" she asked.

"Oh, yes, of course!" I replied without reservation.

"Then study Pythagoras," said Grandma. With that, she was gone.

I sat up in bed, now fully awake. *The triangle guy?* Why

would she want me to read about an ancient mathematician, and how would that help me manifest my long-standing dream of owning a Laguna Beach home? I'd fallen in love with Laguna Beach when I'd first visited Grandma Pearl's oceanside home in that community. I had instantly connected with the artist-colony feel. The town was devoid of tract houses or chain stores, and it had a charming mixture of quaint bungalows and unique mansions. Everything about Laguna Beach screamed "nonconformist," which appealed to the individualist within me.

I also loved Laguna Beach's rolling beds of wildflowers, which decorated the shoreline. Like chocolate chip cookie dough, the white sandy beaches were dotted with impressive granite rock formations. The beauty and relaxed lifestyle of this little town seemed like a soulful sanctuary amid the rest of Southern California's harried pace.

Motivated by Grandma Pearl's promise of manifesting my dream to live in Laguna Beach, I scrawled "Pythagorus" on my nightstand writing tablet, incorrectly guessing how to spell his name. All I knew about him, which I recalled from my old algebra classes, was that he had somehow calculated the diagonal measurements of triangles.

That morning, I researched Pythagoras on the Internet and discovered that he was a philosopher and spiritual teacher as well as a mathematician. He practiced, and advocated, a completely vegetarian diet, and he taught his students ancient spiritual secrets in caves. I was fascinated, but wasn't sure how this knowledge would impact my living arrangements.

I recalled the dream repeatedly, searching for additional cues. The images of the chairs, as well as my reaction to them, puzzled me. Now that I was awake, the chairs didn't seem familiar at all. They weren't Grandma's chairs, as far as I remembered, yet in the dream, I'd had such a powerful emotional connection to them, as if they held personal significance.

I mentally asked Grandma Pearl and my other angels to help. *What exactly do you want me know about Pythagoras?* I asked them.

As all this was going on, I was also focused on an upcoming trip in which I was scheduled to give a lecture and appear on two television shows. I stood at the bathroom mirror and pushed my hair around. *Hmm,* I thought, *I definitely need to go to the hairdresser and get some help.* But who would I go to? My previous hair stylist hadn't worked out, and I hadn't replaced him yet.

I sat cross-legged on the floor and said to the fairies and angels, *Please guide me to a hairdresser who can truly help me. I would like to find someone who is on the spiritual path, and who is also very good with hair.* Even though, in retrospect, that sounds like an unusual combination to ask for in a hair stylist, it was my true desire. I had learned the importance of making heartfelt prayers, as opposed to asking for "politically correct" assistance.

After mentally saying the prayer, I quietly listened for guidance. I did this by focusing my mind on hearing the reply as a passive instrument, akin to a satellite dish receiving television signals. The angels had taught me this passive method of listening, and they had explained that when we *strain* to hear the voice of heaven, we block ourselves. In fact, they said, anytime that we *push* to make something happen, we're acting out of an underlying fear that it might not happen. That very fear is the reason why our goal eludes us.

I received my reply as a feeling to walk over and retrieve a phone book. Guided to the Yellow Pages, I flipped to the "Beautician" section. One particular ad seemed to glow around the edges, and I instantly knew that the angels and fairies were directing me to that salon.

I walked into my hairdressing appointment two days later, not knowing what to expect. A man in his early 20s named John was the person who had answered the phone when I'd called for an appointment, and I had instantly liked him. As I sat in his chair, he asked me the usual new-client questions. When he inquired about my line of work, I was perfectly honest with him: I told him that I wrote spiritual books.

John stopped talking, causing me to briefly wonder if he was blown away by my reply. He was, but not in the negative sense. "What *kind* of spiritual books?" he asked.

"Books on angels, psychic phenomena, and spiritual growth," I replied. "They're nondenominational, and could probably be categorized as New Age."

"Interesting . . ." was all he said, then he walked away. Mercifully, John returned immediately, before I had a chance to feel awkward. He put two books on my lap, saying, "Here are a couple of books that I've been reading." The subtitle of the top book winked at me knowingly—and I could hardly believe what I was seeing: It was a book about Pythagoras! Of course, I had never mentioned my dream to John or anyone else.

When I inquired about his choice in books, John explained that he had an avid interest in Pythagoras and related topics. I excitedly told him about my Grandma Pearl's message. He said that he was accustomed to being "in the flow" of receiving and giving messages, so he wasn't surprised that we had connected. Over the next month, John gave me written material to help me understand the great philosopher's theories. He also lent me books on Nikola Tesla, the Kabbalah, and numerology. I read each book with joy, acknowledging that my Grandma Pearl was working with heaven to impart crucial information to me.

John's books helped me discover that divination cards, such as Tarot, are based upon Pythagorean and Egyptian theories about "vibrational imprints." These theories say that every number, word, picture—indeed, everything—vibrates at a specific rate or speed. Since our thoughts and emotions are energy transmissions, we tend to attract people, situations, items, and divination cards that complement our thought and feeling patterns.

Grandma Pearl's dream visitation and message about Pythagoras led me to study divination cards and experiment with different decks. I asked Hay House, my publisher, if I could create a deck of angel cards for them. Within one month, they gave me the go-ahead, and I began assembling the artwork for the *Healing with the Angels* Oracle Cards.

Meanwhile, my workshop schedule began to intensify. Occasionally, I admitted to myself that I enjoyed being on the road, away from Michael. I loved talking with spiritually minded people and engaging in deep, philosophical discussions. I believed that if I fulfilled that need during my workshops, I wouldn't be so hungry for it when I returned home.

One day, though, a spiritual teacher and I were having lunch and were discussing how to juggle travel, writing, and family time. She made a profound statement that seemed to travel directly from God's mouth to my ear. She said, "It's inevitable that every trip we take profoundly changes us. When we return home, we are a different person for having gone on that trip. The experiences we have, the sights that we see, the people we meet—they all alter us in deep ways. While we can discuss our trip with our family members who stayed home, the fact is that we come home a different person from the one who left."

I was stunned by the simple truth of her statement. It also chilled me to think that Michael and I were growing farther apart, and that my constant road trips were a factor. I thought of several spiritual teachers whom I'd met who had active touring schedules. Some of their marriages had withstood the strains of separations and road trips, but I'd also witnessed several of my friends' marriages dissolve.

That night, alone in my hotel room, I prayed, "Dear God, I know that You have a plan for my love life. I know that You are supporting me in all ways so that I can fulfill my mission. I am grateful for all of Your help, and I accept it now. You know that I desire great love in my life, and I would love to be with a spiritually minded partner. If Michael and I are meant to be together, please guide us to heal our marriage. If we are not meant to be together, please help me to know for sure. Thank you."

❀ ❀ ❀

CHAPTER 6

Incarnated Elementals

My plane landed early the next morning at Orange County's John Wayne Airport. As I loaded my luggage into the car, I felt overdue for a nature walk. I'd spent too much time that weekend under ultraviolet lights, breathing recirculated hotel air.

So I headed to the beach to rest, hoping for some clear guidance from my fairy friends. I spread my sweatshirt on a sand dune near the water, forming a makeshift beach blanket. My body felt heavy, and I knew that the fairies were conducting that *Gulliver's Travels*–type healing session on me. Waves of energy lifted from my legs, my back and my shoulders, and around my head.

I felt paralyzed, yet strangely peaceful—considering the fact that an invisible force was pinning me down. The fairies treated me with such gentle love that I instinctively trusted them. I breathed a deep sigh, closed my eyes, and surrendered to the moment.

I noticed a little girl playing in the surf. Her carrot-colored hair bounced as she jumped over each rolling wave. I saw small bright lights surrounding her shoulders, and I tuned in to get a better look at the beings around her. Suddenly, I caught my breath: "She has fairies as guardian angels!"

I held my head, bowled over by the realization that fairies could function in this way. Up until that point, I'd assumed that everyone's guardians were the same: feather-winged angels, deceased loved ones, or both. I didn't realize that a third choice was available. As I watched the girl and her fairies play, I felt a bevy of small beings—the fairies!— gather around my right shoulder.

"Yes," they whispered into my right ear in unison, "you've discovered the next level of truth about spiritual guides. And you're about to learn so much more."

I felt a little intimidated, as if the fairies were flaunting the fact that they knew my future. What? I silently implored. If you know what I'm going to learn in the future, why can't you just tell me now?

"You have to be ready first."

Okay, now the fairies are teasing me, I thought.

Surrounded by Fairies

"I want to know why that girl over there has fairies, instead of angels, surrounding her." The words rang in my ears after I said them aloud, making me aware that I sounded like I was barking orders. I softened my energy, and I felt the fairies respond in kind. They knew that I was only after information, not a power struggle.

"You've used the expression many times: 'Like attracts like,'" the fairies told me. They sounded like one being, nuzzled immediately next to my right ear. The unified voice was a collective consciousness, like a swarm of bees making a singular "buzzzz" sound. I shuddered for a moment at their words, realizing that the fairies had been watching me for some time. I was obviously on full display for all of heaven to watch and comment upon!

Yes, I mentally responded, *we attract people and experiences to us that match our thinking and emotional patterns. If we think negatively, for instance, we tend to attract negative circumstances and pessimistic people.*

"Exactly!" the voice replied. *"And similarly, you attract beings in the spirit world who match your thoughts and feelings. The red-headed girl in the surf has attracted many fairies as her guides because she has the same interests and purpose that they do. We fairies are vitally concerned with environmental causes, yet we also know the importance of purposeful playtime as a way to clear and energize the soul.*

"The girl's life purpose is to help environmental causes, especially marine life. She will study marine biology in college, and will be a vocal advocate for the whales and for ocean cleanliness. We are guarding and guiding her to ensure that she doesn't get off-course, because we desperately need the help of individuals like her."

I watched the etheric beauty of the girl's movements as her willowy body danced gracefully along the surf. *She even* looks *like a fairy!* I mentally commented.

"Exactly!" they replied.

Exactly what? I asked.

"She looks like a fairy because she is one!"

I heard tittering laughter, and I assumed that the fairies were joking with me. They must have observed my reaction, because they spoke in a more serious tone. *"You are among many incarnated elementals for a good reason."*

Reincarnated elementals?

"No, incarnated elementals. Many people are actually members of our culture, incarnated into human bodies. Please understand, though: Everybody's soul—whether they are fairy, human, angel, or animal—looks the same. The soul is a spark of Divine white light, regardless of the physical shell that surrounds it.

"However, each spark of light spends their lifetime in different places. Some souls choose planet Earth, while other souls prefer a different physical or nonphysical location. The energy of that location is eventually imprinted in the energy body—what you call an 'aura'—that surrounds each soul.

"So, the soul takes on the shape and characteristics appropriate to the locale that the soul normally lives in. That is why the red-haired girl looks and acts like a fairy. It is because she has spent many lifetimes as a fairy in the fairy realm. When she elected to incarnate as a human in this lifetime, her energy body molded her physical body into a fairylike form."

My mind was reeling, yet my heart and gut told me that the fairies spoke the truth. *Of course!* I thought. *Fairies who incarnate in human form could have more control over environmental concerns. They could become powerful caretakers of nature and animals, since that is the fairies' chief concern.*

The Lightworkers' Angels

I walked over to a granite rock, my thoughts racing at the implications of incarnated elementals in human form. I found a sun-covered, flat rock with an adjacent stone functioning as a chair back, and I snuggled up to its radiant heat. Seagulls and pelicans followed a fishing boat near the shore, pleading loudly for scraps of fish. I wondered what type of guardian angels worked with the seabirds, and a moment later, I "saw" the answer. Once again, asking a question triggered the experience of receiving new information.

Around each seabird, I saw wispy, grayish-white beings that looked unlike any guardian angels or fairies I'd ever seen. They were wingless and apparently armless, or else their arms were pressed flat against their sides. About three inches long, they looked like stretched torsos with small heads.

"They're called 'sprites,'" I heard the fairies say, interrupting my thoughts. I watched sunbathers relaxing on their beach blankets, and for a moment, I felt envious that they could simply relax and enjoy themselves on the beach. My time, in contrast, seemed to be completely devoted to Socratic dialogues with fairies. Could I have no privacy? No time off for good behavior?

"Sprites are cousins to us," the fairies continued, oblivious to my irritation at their intrusion into my thoughts. *"Their role in the elemental kingdom is to watch over all bodies of water, including lakes, rivers, streams, ponds, and the ocean. They act as 'guardian angels' to all animals, fish, and birds who live in or near water. Sprites are a very important member of our clan, and humans who care about the water environment can send their blessings and pledges of assistance to sprites."*

The fairies' beautiful words and energy helped me let go of my annoyance at being in a fishbowl, with angels and fairies entering my private thoughts. *"We understand you, Doreen,"* they said with a powerful reassurance that took my breath away.

What do they understand about me? I wondered.

"*We work with Archangel Michael, who oversees all light-workers, and he has asked us to teach you some vital information so that you may pass it along to those who need it. They will be guided to your writings or workshops, sometimes without knowing why, so that you might dispense these teachings. As you know, much of your work involves teaching other spiritual healers and teachers, who in turn pass the information along to their own clients or students. It's very important that this information be shared at this time in human history.*"

Now my irritation was completely replaced by a new sense of intrigue. What would the fairies teach me?

🌸 🌸 🌸

CHAPTER 7

The New Age of Peace

I heard the fairies giggling among themselves, and in my mind's eye, I saw them huddled in a conference. Intuitively, I knew that they were debating the best strategy for relaying information to me.

"We feel that you are ready to hear most of the truth right away," their collective voice said to me. The voice was unified, strong, and powerful—yet it was also quiet, like a forceful whisper.

"We shall withhold some information, and instead orchestrate experiences that will convey the same information to you directly. We feel that you may not believe some of the information if we merely tell it to you. However, if you

experience it for yourself, we know that you will have a deeper understanding of what we are asking you to teach others."

Fair enough, I responded, as if shaking hands in a contract negotiation. *I'll tell you honestly if I don't understand something that you're teaching me.*

"We understand that characteristic about you, Doreen," they replied with love in their collective voice. *"That's why you are receiving a large share of our communications: precisely because you're open to it, and are also open to giving honest feedback if you don't understand something. You also have shown great courage in speaking your truth publicly."*

Well, I feel that I still have much more to learn and more to teach, but thank you.

"Yes, and we will help you reach a wider audience in a very short period of time," they replied. *"These teachings MUST reach as many people as possible, as quickly as possible."*

I'm open and very curious about what you are going to teach me, I told them. *When do we begin?*

Messages for Lightworkers

"We begin now," the fairies explained, *"but first we must prepare your body to receive these messages, for on a deep level, you already know this information. So please inhale some air very deeply, and then exhale completely and slowly. Keep repeating this deep and slow breathing while you listen to our teachings. The breath will help infuse the information deep into your cells so that your body will magnetize it as new programming. This will accelerate your learning schedule, compressing the amount of time it will take you to assimilate this information.*

"Rather than informing you, we are helping you to remember what you previously learned prior to this incarnation. This is

deep-seated programming that you agreed to and approved of prior to your incarnation to help you remember and fulfill your life's mission. All lightworkers have such programming.

"Deep within lightworkers' hearts and guts, they have a sense of time urgency. This feeling calls on the lightworker to help the world in a spiritual way, and to do so immediately. Most lightworkers are aware that they are 'different' from others. They are extremely sensitive individuals who have been teased for being 'too sensitive,' 'weird,' or ' know-it-alls.' They suffer from the physical symptoms common to most lightworkers, including an intermittent ringing sound in one ear."

I've had that ringing sound in my right ear most of my life! I said. *What is it?*

"Two-fold: First, it is a tone designed to keep your spiritual frequency level higher than the material plane and race-mind consciousness."

What? I asked for clarification.

"Think of a smog layer over the earth, but imagine that instead of air pollution, it is a collection of fear-based thoughts. It consists of all of the anger felt during morning commutes to work, plus stress from 'lack thoughts,' where humans believe they lack the money, love, or time that they need. These negative energies clog the dense level hugging the earth. And yes, you are correct in wondering whether it has a detrimental effect on everyone on the planet, including Mother Earth herself.

"If lightworkers lived and breathed this 'smog,' which we call 'race-mind consciousness,' they would become depressed and incapable of helping to eradicate it. So the heavenly supporters to lightworkers—including the archangels, master healers, teachers, elementals, and starpeople—send strong bands of lightwaves to the lightworkers. It is usually received in one ear as a high-pitched tone that can seem loud, and even painful. This tone elevates the body's frequency above the race-mind consciousness, so the lightworker

can retain a pool of energy and hopefulness that will motivate him or her to contribute toward the solution."

Oh, that makes a lot of sense, I responded. Now, you also mentioned that the ringing in the ears was a two-fold process. What's the other part?

"The ringing also comes from a 'downloading,'—as you'd call it these days—of information. It's much like your computer's modem making a ringing sound as it is connecting. We send you updates of information related to your lightworker mission. A great deal of this information is based on fourth-dimensional teachings, so it wouldn't make sense if we simply told all of you about it. Instead, we bypass the intellect and send the information in a tonal system straight into your unconscious and heart chakra. That way, you incorporate this new programming into your daily thoughts and behavior."

Oh, that sounds like mind control! I protested. (I was always the freedom fighter.) This discussion reminded me of a bad science fiction movie. Besides, my rock chair was beginning to feel uncomfortable, so I decided to lie down on the sand. Of course the fairies didn't skip a beat in following me with their presence and their teachings.

"We understand the fear of being controlled," the fairies said empathically. "We also understand the human's ego fears. The ego doesn't want you to engage in lightwork because it wants the earth to stay choked with fear."

Why would the ego want that? I was baffled.

"Because the ego is 100 percent pure fear! If you lose your fear, the ego has lost its life force. If you help other people lose their fear, the ego has lost its power base in the human race. So the ego will do everything possible to distract you from your mission and make you feel afraid and powerless.

"But please understand that you lightworkers contracted with us in heaven to continually remind you of your mission. You knew, *before incarnation, that you'd go off the path occasionally. You asked us to nudge you during those times. So we aren't violating your free will; we're just fulfilling our contract with you lightworkers."*

I knew the truth of their statements deep within my heart and gut, so I listened open-mindedly as the fairies continued.

"The lightworkers have incarnated during this important shift in humanity. Under the watchful guidance of Archangel Michael, you lightworkers are eradicating the world of the effects of fear. You are also helping to reduce the amount of fear and negative energy released into the earth's atmosphere. You lightworkers have a front-line mission, which first involves stopping the fear habit yourself, and then modeling or teaching others to do the same."

How do we do that? I wondered. *That sounds like a lofty ambition!* I felt a bit overwhelmed.

Truth and Telepathy

"Oh, you have plenty of support that far exceeds the power of any fear," the fairies said reassuringly. *"And the increasing numbers of people who are praying and following spiritual practices has certainly helped. Fear will leave the planet when you return to a telepathic basis of living."*

Excuse me?

"At one time, in a place called Lemuria, humans didn't rely on the spoken or written word to communicate with one another. All exchanges were done on a mind-to-mind basis. You would think a thought and another would receive it, in much the same way a verbal conversation is carried on today. Lemuria was completely peaceful, and truly a model of Eden, the paradise that many of you lightworkers remember on a deep, unconscious basis. Part of the driving motivation for lightworkers is to return to an Earthly paradise because of their Lemurian memories.

"In Lemuria, all communication was telepathic. Even today, everyone is capable of being telepathic, but most humans deny these impulses. They either block out all conscious awareness of their psychic impressions, or they convince themselves that it is their imagination. Instead of relying on their inner truth, they lean on outer sources. This leads to the illusion of scarcity, because it seems that you have to go outside yourself to capture your material needs.

"If humans would just uncover the rich treasures that exist within themselves, including the endless supply of material and spiritual wealth that they currently hold, they could never be afraid again. If humans would allow themselves to psychically discern the many angels and spirit guides that surround them, they could never feel alone or friendless again. If humans would be unafraid of seeing their beloved deceased ones, they would instantly lose all fear of death.

"Your role is to teach telepathic development courses far and wide. Teach as many people as possible about the power of their telepathic minds. Many of your students, as well as other teachers, will also disseminate this information. You mustn't fear or doubt your mission—ever. You and all the other lightworkers are vitally needed for this mission now."

Yes, I think I understand. But please tell me: Why is it so important to teach psychic development? I asked.

"In order for humans to get away from their scarcity thinking, they must begin to rely upon their telepathic minds. As they follow their inner guidance, all of their physical and emotional needs will automatically be met. And here is one of the most important components of the plan: When humans return to telepathic communication, dishonesty will leave the planet."

How so? I queried.

"The only reason why lies go unrecognized now is because humans deny their gut feelings that tell them that 'something is wrong.' As humans become more telepathic, they will no longer disguise or distrust this inner warning system. So in a fairly short time period, lies and half-truths will no longer be tolerated. Just as you can hide nothing from us in the spirit world, so will all untruths be out in the open among humans.

"The young humans, whom you have called 'The Indigo Children,' already have this skill in place. They have inner detectors that smell untruths immediately. Because they are bombarded by many untruths daily, their systems can become overwhelmed. That's when they act-out in protest, sometimes aggressively."

That makes a lot of sense, I said. So when people can no longer lie, what's going to happen to the many institutions and systems that have lies or half-truths at their very core? What will happen to the government, legal, media, educational, medical, and other systems?

"The angels are working with members of these systems to try and heal them from the inside. Many lightworkers are working undercover as employees within these systems. The spirit world is working with humans who work in these systems during their dream times, trying to convince them to live in integrity at home and at work."

And if they don't listen? I asked.

"Then these systems may fall suddenly. If that happens, the role of the lightworker still remains the same: to help people to be unafraid. Your role, in particular, is to help the lightworkers to be unafraid. When lightworkers worry or have fearful thoughts, the Archangel Michael can't clearly communicate with them. He needs his lightworkers to have clear channels of communication so that he can give specific guidance to each one for their part in the overall plan.

"We need you to teach lightworkers how to choose loving, instead of fearful, thoughts. Teach them psychic development skills, and help them to trust their inner guidance. Let them know that it isn't crazy or evil to listen to the voice of heaven. As you do so, Archangel Michael will have an easier time communicating with his 'troops,' the lightworkers."

And how do the fairies fit in with Archangel Michael? I inquired.

"Like you, we work for him. One reason why we help light-workers is because of our common intention of lifting the smog belt of race-mind consciousness that hugs the planet Earth. Since we are the beings of heaven primarily interested in environmental concerns, we want the 'psychic smog' lifted. It chokes Mother Earth and pollutes all of her inhabitants in the plant, geological, animal, and human realms."

❧ ❧ ❧

CHAPTER 8

Dragonflies and Dolphins

The following months seemed like a blur of plane trips and weekend workshops, as I followed Archangel Michael's "orders" and taught psychic development and angel therapy to as many people as possible. I taught one- and two-day courses, and also led a six-day spiritual counseling certification course.

One weekend I was in Virginia Beach, Virginia, teaching this course. This was my third time to the magical area where Edgar Cayce had created his Association for Research and Enlightenment. On Saturday afternoon, I had some free time to take a beach walk. As I sauntered along the white sand, thoroughly enjoying the sunshine and salt air, some movement in the ocean caught my eye.

"Oh!" I exclaimed, as sleek gray dolphins meandered in and out of the waves. Their exquisite gracefulness moved me—it was like watching ballerinas perform. I mentally called out to the dolphins, quickening my pace to keep up with them as they swam parallel to the shore. *Please come closer so that I can swim with you!* I pleaded with them.

I calculated whether I could swim out to them, and decided that they were just a shade too far from the beach for me to reach. They didn't move closer to me, but I did feel a warm swelling in my heart. I had just fallen in love with these dolphins.

The following month, I taught a different group of students who were taking the certification course in New York City. As Archangel Michael had prophesied, I was very happy teaching psychic development courses. I seemed to possess a knack for explaining esoteric concepts in a grounded way, and the majority of my students rapidly became highly psychic.

Meeting the Incarnated Elementals

On Sunday evening, a student named Patricia and I sat in LaGuardia Airport, waiting to board our plane. As we stood in the airport check-in line, she discussed her ambivalence about her present job with a Chicago financial corporation. "I'm not sure whether to retire early or to stay on longer and get more benefits," Patricia said.

Just then, Patricia exclaimed, "Oh, wow! Look at that!"

She pointed to a man wearing a T-shirt with the name and logo of Patricia's Chicago employer. Below the logo, in large letters, the shirt read *Carpe Diem,* which means "seize (or enjoy) the day."

"I've been working at the corporation for many years, and I've never seen that shirt before!" Patricia marveled. "It's a sign; I know it's a sign. Why would I see a T-shirt with my company logo all the way out here in New York, when that company is regional to Chicago only? And on top of that, the shirt tells me to 'seize the day'! Clearly, I'm supposed to take an early retirement and enjoy my life."

As Patricia and I discussed this amazing synchronicity, we both noticed a very odd-appearing man walking past. Dressed in a deep brown burlap shirt tied with a rope, he sported a tall, white hat with a pointy dome, its brims rolled downward. The man's ruddy Celtic face featured a prominently pointy reddish nose.

"Doesn't he look like . . . ?" Patricia sputtered.

"Yes, a gnome!" I excitedly replied

"Oh, my! He looks more like a gnome than any statue or picture I've ever seen." Patricia was stunned. She looked at me and asked, "Do these kinds of things happen to you all the time?"

"Pretty much," I smiled. "I'm going to go over and talk with him. I bet he's an interesting fellow." I felt slightly nervous as I walked over to interview the man. He was slightly reclusive, and not so amenable to inviting me into his space. But with gentle persistence, I learned that he belonged to a religious order akin to the monks, and that he ran a children's care facility. He seemed increasingly comfortable sharing with me, and I listened without interrupting his train of thought.

Then the man excused himself to go to the rest room, and—although our airplane didn't board for another 30 minutes—we never saw him again. Was he a briefly incarnated elemental, sent to show me an extreme example of one? Patricia was instantly convinced of his authenticity, and after spending time with the gentle man, so was I.

One month later, I was back in Virginia, giving a workshop with Nick Bunick. Nick was an Oregon businessman who discovered his past-life connection with Christ, as described in the best-selling book, *The Messengers*. The evening before our workshop, Nick and I were having dinner with several others at a large restaurant. Among our dining companions were several graduates of my six-day spiritual counseling training program. We were all engrossed in conversation when a man who walked into the restaurant caught our eyes. He wore green pants and a green print shirt, and although he wasn't technically "tall," his thin body gave the appearance of being long and lanky. Walking with a rubbery gait, he sat at his table with a posture that announced that he was eating dinner alone.

"Oh my God!" one of the graduate students announced. "That man is covered with leprechauns!"

I looked over and saw verifiable evidence of her exclamation. Dozens of tiny leprechaun spirit guides busily surrounded the man. The imps were engaged in hyperactive mischief, and those of us who practiced clairvoyance watched in fascination.

"Look, two of the leprechauns are peering inside the man's brandy snifter!" said one student.

"Oh, no, one fell in the brandy!" another blurted out.

"And look at those other leprechauns—they're peeking up the waitress's skirt!" laughed another student.

We all giggled at the antics of the leprechauns surrounding the man, who seemed oblivious to all the activity.

"Did you notice that the man himself has all the appearance of a leprechaun, too?" I asked, recalling the fairies' lessons about incarnated elementals.

"Yes, you're right. He does look exactly like a lep-rechaun!"one of the students chimed in.

I made a mental note to ask the fairies for more information about incarnated elementals. Between seeing the "gnome" at LaGuardia and now a "leprechaun" in Virginia, I was losing all skepticism concerning the matter.

Tones of Healing and Peace

The next day, I walked to a marshy area next to the conference hotel. Sitting by a blue-black lake, I noticed dragonflies darting among the lily pads and frogs. The majestic willow trees were the perfect backdrop for this lovely scene, and I felt great peace and love in my heart as I called out to the fairies to further explain the nature of the incarnated elementals.

"Many of the lightworkers here among us in human form do not actually have human origin," I heard an echoey voice say. I looked over to the pond and it almost seemed as if the voice was emanating from a large dragonfly.

Reading my thoughts, the fairies noted: *"Our voices are not actually coming from the dragonfly, but we wanted to give you another example of an incarnated elemental. The dragonflies and frogs are from our kingdom, and they are helping to transmute stress from Mother Earth. One reason why frogs are so prominently featured in fairy tales is that the human heart recognizes the magic of the elemental kingdom.*

"Frogs, being close to earth and water, absorb much of Earth's densest and harshest energy, yet frogs exhibit no signs of stress, fear, or anger. They stand steady, because they know that their mission is to chant deep baritone music as an incantation to ward away

stress. *Their toning actually transmutes stress from their own bodies, as well as the earth and water bodies they inhabit. The dragonflies work in concert with the frogs, like tiny angels carrying the weight off the frogs' backs and into the etheric atmosphere. Their wings hum a steady droning sound that transmutes negativity. There is a therapeutic benefit to listening to the tones of frogs and dragonflies."*

I watched as the dragonflies circled around the frogs' backs, while the frogs gazed steadily ahead, chanting their steady drumbeat of tones without interruption. I marveled at how similar the dragonfly wings were to the wings of the fairies I had seen.

"That's because we're from the same kingdom," I heard the fairies remark. Would I ever grow accustomed to being in a fishbowl, where all of my thoughts were on public display to the spirit world? Then I remembered Archangel Michael's prophecy of how we'd soon all be telepathic, rendering private, dishonest thoughts impossible.

"The bravest of the fairies decide to incarnate into the physical world, both to experience this dimension, and also to make a great impact on environmental protection."

What do you mean? I asked.

"Well, most fairies are absolutely joyous, happy-go-lucky beings. We know how to create—or as you say, 'manifest'—all of our supply. Basically, we just draw to us, out of the ethers, anything that matters to us. We can binge upon life freely.

"We have no idea why humans feel that they have to destroy environmental resources in order to have their basic needs for clothing, food, and shelter met. Don't humans realize that they can merely think a thought and create whatever it is that they need? Apparently not, for we watch in horror and terror as human beings snarl the environment with harsh machinery, pesticides, and waste matter.

"So, many of the elementals volunteer to incarnate into the

physical world. Those who aren't ready to function in the role of humans take care of the intermediate tasks performed by frogs or dragonflies.

"To tell the truth, it's usually those elementals who are most disgusted with the human race's disregard for the environment who end up volunteering to become disguised as humans, so the elementals manifest the condition of becoming incarnated into a human body. First, they must visualize and sense what it must be like to become human. Then, they must seal this visualization with a kiss, meaning that their hearts must extend outwardly in a visible line leading to the effects of the manifestation. In other words, they must feel love surrounding the proposed project.

"All elementals know that once you cast this spell, there's no turning back from the manifestation. It must *occur, in some way or the other. The fairies aren't concerned with how the manifestation will occur, they just know without doubt, that it will happen."*

Elemental Characteristics

After an elemental decides to manifest as an incarnate human, what happens next? I inquired.

"Much like a human birth, two parents are selected. The incarnated elemental is born in a normally human way. In fact, the being usually develops amnesia about their celestial origins. All they know is that they are angry with other people over the mistreatment of animals and the environment.

"For that reason, many incarnated elementals are raucous practical jokers. They are acting-out a low-level aggression, the same anger that fueled their desire to incarnate in the first place."

How interesting! I noted. *What other characteristics do incarnated elementals share in common?*

"Most are of Celtic origin, or have a Celtic appearance," was

the melodic reply. *"Ruddy complexions and red-hued or lighter hair is common among us. All the elementals tend to share a suspicious nature concerning humans from decades of watching them impinge upon the earth's environment, cruelly killing its plants and animals. So we tend to have a watch-and-see attitude toward them.*

"All elementals—whether incarnated or not—can sense when a human sincerely cares about the environment, and we are absolutely loyal toward such people. We try to teach other humans to treat Mother Nature with absolute respect. When they don't, that's when we become upset. And that's why the elementals have earned the reputation of being mean or mischievous. We just cannot hide our indignation when we see humans polluting the land or mistreating the animals. Could you?"

No, I'm like you, I admitted. *I get really upset when I see litter on the ground and when I read about the incredible cruelty involved in factory-farming animals for food and leather.*

"Of course you become upset. All members of the elemental kingdom do."

I gasped. *Are you saying that I'm an incarnated elemental?*

"It's not up to us to tell you, or anyone, which realm they originated from. What we can do, though, is tell you about the different types of incarnations that lightworkers commonly originate from. Then you can decide for yourself!"

My mind swam with thoughts and feelings about the possibility that I was a member of this magical clan. Could it be true? I thought back to my actions as a child: how I'd started a movement at my junior high school to enlist support for the wild mustangs, who were being slaughtered and mistreated. I'd even given a talk at the local Sierra Club about the mustangs when I was just 13 years old. So my environmental activism certainly fit the bill of "incarnated elemental" characteristics. And I was of Celtic origin, with Irish genetics and red-hued hair. Even my first name was Irish, and so were most of my friends!

"Elementals do tend to affiliate with one another. Another characteristic among all elementals is a love of playfulness and music. They also usually choose Earth signs astrologically."

Well, those three characteristics certainly fit me. What do you mean, though, about choosing Earth signs astrologically?

"The soul's birth time is precalculated prior to incarnation to give the being the maximum support for their life's work and mission. You chose to be a Taurean woman in this life to stay grounded, very close to the earth. As a spiritual teacher, it's essential that you remain grounded so that you can teach practical messages that make sense and are applicable to daily life here."

That makes sense, I replied. *But what about my need—my absolute requirement—to live near the ocean? I appreciate the mountains and the desert, but I could never live away from the water.*

"Each elemental is assigned to different parts of the earth's custodianship program. There are elementals who must live in the mountains, others who must live in the desert, and still others— like you—who must live near a large body of water. It is in your character makeup, because it is your assignment."

To help the ocean? I asked.

"Yes, and its inhabitants. Each lightworker has a specific purpose. The incarnated elementals are in charge of stewardship of Mother Nature. And there are lightworkers who have incarnated from other realms as well."

Like what? I had moved completely away from skepticism into an open-minded dialogue.

"As we said to you previously, all souls are identical on the inside, each being a spark of Divine white light. Yet, as we just discussed, the soul takes on the physical or etheric body that will best serve their life's mission. Beings with similar characteristics and missions tend to bond with one another, and we call these groups of similar beings 'realms,' or 'kingdoms.'

"We've been focusing on the 'elemental kingdom,' which consists of the fairies, pixies, gnomes, brownies, leprechauns, mene-huene [Hawaiian spirituality's equivalent of our fairies], *sprites, dragonflies, frogs, tree and bush people, mermaids, dolphins, and minerals. Yet, there are other kingdoms who take on a human body so that they may focus on a specific project on Earth. These include the angelic and starpeople realms."*

Diverse Origins

I don't understand, I responded. *You're saying that there are people who have incarnated from the angelic realms as well?*

"'Incarnated angels' are those beings who have taken on a semi-human form to impact the material world from this dense level. Some angels incarnate briefly to, for instance, rescue a human who is in trouble. Other angels incarnate for one or more lifetimes."

Do they have distinguishing characteristics, like the incarnated elementals do? Are there ways to tell if someone is an incarnated angel or not? I asked.

"Oh my, yes. Just like the incarnated fairies look *like fairies, and the incarnated leprechauns* look *like leprechauns, so do the incarnated angels* look *like angels. They are men, women, and children of extraordinary beauty, with sweet heart-shaped faces and cupid lips.*

"They tend to be heavy-set, or struggle with their weight, because this Earth environment is among the harshest in the galaxy system. Angels tend to put weight on their Earthly bodies to buffer themselves from the negative energy upon the planet, and also because they absorb negative energy from others, since incarnated angels usually put themselves in Earthly situations that promote the absorption of negative energy.

"They become professional helpers, working as nurses, teachers,

flight attendants, therapists, and such. Even if they are not employed as helpers, incarnated angels are put in the position of 'helper' frequently. Strangers pour out their hearts to incarnated angels, saying, 'There's just something about you that makes me feel that I can trust you.' Of course there is! Incarnated angels see the very best in everyone, and it makes a person feel wonderful to talk to such a being.

"Yet the flip side for the incarnated angels is that their love lives are often in shambles, as they fall in love with everyone they meet. Therefore, angels may marry humans who are technically 'inappropriate partners' simply because the angels can see the potential within these people and vow to help change them into ideal mates."

You said that incarnated elementals are usually beings with astrological earth signs. What about incarnated angels? Do they have similar patterns? I asked.

"They are frequently fire signs," the fairies replied, "yet we also see angels come from the other astrological signs less frequently. So an incarnated angel could be an earth, water, or air sign. However, the air signs are usually the 'starpeople.'"

It sounds like you're talking about E.T.'s, I remarked.

"The truth is that starpeople are 'extra-terrestrial,' meaning that they haven't been on earth much, if ever. Many starpeople are here for the first time, and they may have buffered their souls by 'borrowing' past-life memories from a human's Akashic records. That way, their souls are cushioned against feeling the impact of the earth's harshness."

Is it really that harsh here on Earth? I asked.

"Oh my goodness, yes!" the fairies exclaimed. "Poor soul, you've forgotten."

Forgotten?

"Before incarnation, most souls are intimidated about coming here, knowing that they're in for an energy-crushing experience.

The purpose is to learn to manage the energy here through the process of service and conscious manifestation in order to create heaven on Earth.

"The starpeople may have the most difficulty with Earth incarnations, though, of all the different realms. This planet is among the most psychologically and physically violent of all locations in the galaxies. Starpeople who incarnate spend their lifetime shaking their heads, wondering how humans can be so cruel to one another. Yet that is precisely why *the starpeople incarnate into human form. Their life purpose is to defuse and transmute anger among Earth's residents, to prevent additional violence, and especially to avoid the* ultimate *act of violence—nuclear war.*

Starpeople have life purposes to 'help as needed,' committing thoughtful and kind acts without regard for their own recognition or reward. By being the 'nice guy or gal,' starpeople smooth the feathers of earthlings so that their overall stress level is reduced. Starpeople understand the ripple effect of a kind act, and they know the major contributions and impact that benevolent acts can have on a planet.

"Advanced civilizations understand the other type of ripple effect, too, where if one planet explodes, its impact rips through entire galaxies. So it's natural that beings who inhabit nearby planets would intervene into Earth's current fork in the road."

Fork in the road?

"Yes," the fairies continued. *"You are at an intersection in your personal and planetary history. There are several alternative futures available to you, which means that you could experience any number of outcomes in the next few years. We in the spirit world are all urging humanity toward the adoption of a natural and peaceful existence."*

Purposeful Direction

What do you mean? I asked the fairies.

"*We'll save that lesson for another time,*" the fairies said in unison. At times, I didn't know if they were speaking or singing to me, their voices were so melodic.

"*Right now, we would really like it if you would help our friends, the seagulls. We'll direct you if you'd like; we simply need you to agree that you'll help them.*"

Of course! I said without a second thought. *I love seagulls. Just show me what you need me to do.*

I didn't hear any directives, but I felt a strong inner urging to walk in a northerly direction along the beach. As if I were being guided by a strong dog on a leash, I continued walking steadily. Around a bend, I saw a huge gathering of seagulls. They strutted elegantly along the seashore, searching for lunchtime sand crabs by drilling with their beaks into the sand's edge.

I could feed them, I mentally noted to myself, wondering if *that* was my assignment. Then I watched in horror as three young boys came screaming down a beach trail with their arms flailing, their voices louder than the crashing surf. They laughed as their raucous shouts and wild behavior obviously startled the seagulls. The birds, not surprisingly, scattered into the air, unnerved by all the commotion.

I watched as the boys scrunched their faces in angry determination, seemingly intent on chasing every seagull off the beach. *Why would anyone want to frighten a bird?* I wondered.

"*Part of your purpose is to help the sea animals,*" I heard the fairies say.

But what am I to do? I asked earnestly.

"*Speak up! Educate people about the ocean environment!*" The fairies sounded practically disgusted, as if their answers should have been obvious to anyone.

My thoughts were interrupted by the sound of the boys tearing into the sand with pounding feet. Each time they did so, the remaining seagulls would momentarily watch the boys, seemingly forgiving their previous actions. The birds were so accustomed to tourists feeding them that they apparently couldn't believe that these small humans could harbor violent intentions.

Finally, I couldn't take it anymore. "Excuse me!" I said loudly and firmly, walking toward the boys. The tallest boy looked at me with an irritated expression on his face.

"Can I ask you a question?" I said, when I was within five feet of him.

He shrugged as a reply. That was enough for me. With my heart pumping from indignation and nervousness, I said, "Why would you want to frighten the seagulls?"

He shrugged again, and his companions looked down.

"The seagulls are our friends, and it's wrong to scare them," I said authoritatively. The boy's eyes revealed that he'd heard me. I talked with the boys further, and when I walked away, I wondered if my actions would have any impact.

That afternoon at home, I composed a letter to the editor of our local newspaper on behalf of the fairies and the seagulls. I wrote a letter to parents, asking them to supervise their children's actions when they were around animals and birds. After all, I wrote, studies show that violent adults usually have childhood histories of violence toward animals. Two days later, the newspaper published my letter, and I received calls from many people who read it.

"*Very good,*" said the fairies. "*Very good.*"

CHAPTER 9

Healing and Manifesting with the Elementals

My travels were taking me all over the United States and Canada, where I'd give workshops to audiences at expos, conferences, and church groups. *The Lightworker's Way* and *Angel Therapy* had both been well received critically and popularly, which led to additional speaking engagements.

I started teaching people about the fairies and the other members of the elemental kingdom. At first, I gingerly introduced these beings to audience members. After all, many people at my workshops believed in angels, but not all of them were ready to hear about fairies. I found that many people of the Christian persuasion thought angels were Divine beings, but believed that fairies were dark and occultlike.

"Fairies are God's nature angels," I taught my audiences.

One time, a woman approached me following a workshop. "I'm a retired Catholic nun," she said, holding my hand with love shining in her eyes. "I just want to thank you for helping me to accept fairies. I never thought of them as being part of God's kingdom until you pointed it out to me."

"They are as much God's creations as any of the angels or people," I replied, giving her a hug.

Seeing the Fairies

Frequently, I'd teach classes devoted to psychic development. In Scottsdale, Arizona, during one such class, I took the students outside so they could see fairies for themselves. We walked to a large bank of flowering shrubs.

"Squint your eyes slightly," I instructed. "and soften your focus and gaze, almost like you were looking at one of those three-dimensional pictures that pop out at you. Look past the flowers. Hold the intention of seeing fairies. Be aware of any doubts or fears in your mind. If you notice any negative intentions or thoughts, mentally call upon the angels to help you release these blocks.

"You'll see, in your mind's eye, streaks of white light jumping from flower to flower. The fairies jump about like fireflies. They're two to three inches long, sometimes shorter and sometimes taller. At first, you'll probably just see their energy, which is the white light that you'll see flitting from flower to flower. Try turning your head and looking at the flowers out of the corner of your eye, also. Sometimes our clairvoyance works better peripherally, because we're more relaxed and open to seeing the spirit world from the corners of our eyes. The front of the eye often strains and thinks too hard, in contrast.

"Initially, you'll probably see the fairies as transparent apparitions in your mind's eye. You may worry that you're inventing these visions, but one of the reasons why children see fairies so often is that they aren't worried whether their visions are imaginary or not. Only the adult ego worries about making mistakes. So, be as a child, and give yourself permission to see the fairies.

"Be patient with yourself and take your time. Remember that the fairies are shy, and they can read your thoughts and emotions. They may not reveal themselves to you immediately. You may have to take some time to earn the fairies' trust before they allow you to see them. Fairies are wary of humans who have impure motivations; or who are brash, rude, or abusive to the environment, so they may need to get to know you first. Mentally talk to the fairies and tell them of your desire to see and work with them. They will help you if they sense that you are a loving soul who desires to help them with environmental concerns.

"After a week or two of communing with nature, and holding the intention to see and hear fairies, you should be able to see them. Eventually, you'll see detailed visions of fairies. Most likely, you'll see the fairies simultaneously in your mind's eye and outside your head. You'll actually see the fairies circling the flowers, plants, animals, and some people—especially incarnated elementals."

A majority of the students were able to see the fairies using these instructions. I was heartened to hear them say to each other, "Ooh, I see them!" and "Wow, they really do move around like fireflies!"

The Tree and Bush People

When I wasn't giving seminars, I was at home in Dana Point, creating a deck of divination cards about angels. The week after returning from Scottsdale, I was in the midst of contacting artists who could illustrate the various meanings of the cards. The selection process was going very well, practically effortlessly. As each new piece of artwork would arrive at my home, I'd study and meditate upon it until the piece "spoke" to me and let me know its meaning.

The *Healing with the Angels* oracle card deck consists of 44 cards, based on the number sequence, "44" or "444," which means (in numerology), "The angels would like to communicate with you." I'd assembled 44 beautiful angel pictures, and was in the process of writing the accompanying guidebook, which would provide basic instructions for interpreting the cards and giving an angel reading.

I continued my daily walks to the Dana Point beach, strolling along the path of the "headlands," a vacant area filled with wild flowers and overgrown bushes. I'd frequently see the "tree people" and "bush people" along the path. These are large spiritual beings who fill the space of a tree or a bush. It's fairly easy to see these beings—they look like large faces with big eyes and prominent noses, jutting out of a tree or bush. The trick is to trust the vision and not wonder whether it's your imagination.

At first, these beings simply watched me walk by. I was being tested in a way, as they wanted to see if I was trustworthy and consistent. Perhaps because I picked up trash from the ground in front of them frequently, I soon began receiving intuitive messages from the tree and bush people.

They were jolly beings with big hearts. I could hear their voices, which had a (not surprisingly) hollow, wooden sound.

Both male and female tree and bush people began speaking to me on my daily walks. I learned that each tree and bush has one primary being inhabiting it. The being seems to be one with the plant; however, the plant has a separate life force from the being. So, a tree being isn't the tree's personality. Rather, the tree being is more like its guardian angel.

On one sunny weekday morning, I walked along the path connecting the headlands with Salt Creek Beach Park. One friendly bush, with a loving grin made by its branches and leaves, attracted my attention. As I stood looking at the bush and its inhabiting bush person, I heard it say, *"We bush and tree people are the living, breathing spirit of the plant's essence."*

Wow! I thought. *That was really a clear communication.* I sat next to the bush, with pen and paper in hand, and asked the bush person to dictate its message to me.

"We emanate what flourishes. The branches and roots are akin to your elemental body: contained but flowing—an outgrowth of the physical sun's energy. Our essence, or spirit or soul, as you call it, is an outgrowth of the Divine sun. One is the material sun, and one is the spiritual sun. Our physical incarnations are the meeting of Spirit and matter."

As I listened and wrote, I noticed fairies dancing through the bush's small, white flowers. *"You see how I have fairies dancing through my branches,"* the bush person continued. *"They are gathering information to draw from, and they are assessing me like tiny physicians. Fairies bring balance to physical bodies of all forms. They adjust and calibrate the 'aura,' which is the energy in-between Spirit and matter.*

"So you might say that the elemental kingdom works on the bridge between Spirit and matter. The fairies are part of the bridge. In a sense, they are *the bridge."*

Messages from the Plant Spirits

I could feel immense gratitude from the bush, as well as the neighboring bush people and fairies. It occurred to me to mentally ask the bush person, *What would you like people to know about you and the other bush and tree people?*

"*The lives of our physical bodies—what you know as trees, bushes, and plants—are very precarious, depending so much upon you humans. We are interdependent upon one another, you depending upon us for shelter, oxygen, sustenance, and such—and we depending upon you to nurture us in return. We are each other's caretakers.*

"*Like you, our spiritual essence is immortal. It is impossible to kill the spirit of a tree, or of any life form, for that matter, but you can wound the heart of a tree by not giving us tree or bush people our just accord. Feed us—not just with your plant fertilizers—but also with your friendship. We are akin to your animal friends, and we need companionship and emotional nurturing as much as they do.*

"*We seek to bond with the human race and all who hear this call; we invite you to come meet with us.* How do you do this? *you may wonder. Simply attune your mind by deciding that you'd like to contact us. You don't need to be physically present with us, since we can feel your energy and are deeply affected by it. Yet, for your benefit—and because we would like to form friendships with you—we invite you to sit, lie down, or simply* be *next to us. Sit on us if you'd like.*

"*Then, throw any thought or question at us that suits your fancy. This is a magical time in your human history. The energy mass has reached its peak and is now resting toward the other side of the bell curve, toward more spiritual inclinations. In other words, the focus on materiality is nearly over, which is just in the nick of time, as many resources are nearly exhausted.*

"You all have reached your peak capacity as consumers, and you are now all sliding back down the scale toward a new evolution of consciousness—one that will have mass appeal. Together, we can help to anchor in this new Dawning Light.

"Hold, in your heart and mind, the intention of spiritually 'adopting' one of us in the elemental plant life kingdom. Each person and their match in the plant kingdom, like soulmates, will find one another and forge a deep and lasting friendship based on mutual caretaking.

"We have much to learn from one another. First, we will help to magnify the human heart's capacity for caring. We can do this without causing hurt, for we work to multiply the prisms of love, deep love. You will see many images of rainbows in the coming weeks, months, and years, as messages that we appreciate being heard, being loved, and being tended to."

A Healing from a Tree Person

I lay down on a bed of grass; soft, decayed branches; and sandy dirt next to the bush. I could feel the bush person's love and gratitude hugging me. Even the spiders seemed joyful. I realized that, just like us, the plant kingdom and its inhabitants simply want to be acknowledged and loved.

I then got up and started picking up some fast-food soda containers and other litter that was strewn among the bushes. The elementals advised me to leave the paper trash on the ground and to focus on cleaning away the plastic debris.

I walked to a bank of wild trees near the Salt Creek Beach Park. They had beautifully thick and tangled underbrush, unlike the artificially manicured trees that inhabit most parks. I crouched as I walked beneath the low-slung branches of a tree that particularly attracted me. The chestnut-colored underbrush was pushed back like a bed comforter, and I nestled upon its welcoming cushion.

I felt myself covered with a large air-pressure mass, like I was flying at a high altitude. It was a familiar feeling that always signaled Spirit's presence to me. Of course, Spirit is everywhere, but there's a sense of great pockets of air pressure wherever a strong spiritual presence exists. I notice it especially where the elementals live. As I sat beneath the tree, I saw and felt images of sadness and anger, stemming from my love life. I saw visions of every man who hadn't appreciated me or who had ignored me. The air pressure grew tighter around my head.

Then the tree person said in a kind, grandfatherly voice, *"My energy is amplifying the feelings you have lodged, unhealed in your heart. Let these feelings come to the surface so that I can help you to release them."*

I gratefully allowed the tree person to be my spiritual healer, and I gave my heart full reign to feel and heal. My chest lurched upward, and I saw a mental movie, like a life review, of my romantic relationships. Every feeling I'd ever stuffed, every cry I'd ever muted, and every tear I'd held back, flowed to the surface. The pain was held inside like frozen teardrops, and the tree person's love was melting it. The unspoken feelings were unexpressed energy that needed to be let out of the starting gate so that they could gallop freely.

I relived a lifetime of unexpressed pain. There was Steven, the cute boy-next-door on Craner Avenue. I'd had such a huge crush on him, but because I was much younger than he was, Steven never paid me any notice. I had a freeze-frame photograph of him in my mind that symbolized my unrequited crush: It was the memory of Steven standing on a grassy mound next to his apartment building's swimming pool. He wore cut-off shorts and was barefoot. He had no idea, I suppose, that I was watching him at that moment, because he stared off into the distance. Steven seemed to be in his own world.

As if I were reviewing my entire life's romantic moments, I next saw a mental movie of Bill, my first boyfriend. Midway through our romance, Bill's family decided he was too young to go steady. A succession of romantic liaisons had all followed, each permeated with disappointment and pain, including my marriage to Michael.

I wondered: Could my unrequited crush on Steven have set the tone for my ensuing love life? Or was it because my father and I weren't that close emotionally? Perhaps I hadn't been choosy enough with romantic partners. I saw that, throughout my life, I had never given up hope that "he"— the man of my dreams—a spiritual, romantic, loving, fun, and committed partner—was out there somewhere.

As the tree person drew each image out of my heart's memory bank, I felt the accompanying crushing disappointment of every relationship I'd had. I cried with relief as the pain was extracted, like a homeopathic tincture drawing out a snake's poisonous venom. When the storm fire of healing energy was over, I lay panting with exhaustive peace. My heart felt completely soft and open, and I emanated great love toward my new friends, the tree and bush people.

The Fairies' Manifestation Secrets

"We want to share our secrets of manifestation with you."

What? I must have fallen asleep, because the fairies' statement startled me.

"How do you think we get our needs met?" the fairies

continued. *"We don't have stores or factories, yet we have plenty of clothing, food, and musical instruments. The answer is that we manifest anything and everything that we need, and we want to teach you to do the same. If you can teach the other people our manifestation secrets, then they won't need to destroy Earth's natural resources to make things. They can simply create them out of thin air, like we do!"*

With all due respect and appreciation for your kind offer, I said, *are your manifestations real, or are they figments of your imagination?* I thought of the many stories of people who had traveled to fairy glens and who had filled their pockets with gold coins from the fairies. Then, when they returned to the human realm, the gold was gone.

Reading my thoughts, the fairies said patiently, *"The gold was real in our dimension, but it didn't translate to the denser realm of the human world. Its energy isn't visible in your world, just like we aren't visible to most people's untrained eyes. When we fairies manifest, it is within our own dimension, and the items match our spiritual frequency. We will teach you to manifest at your own level so that the situations, people, and items will seem quite real to you."*

But I only want to manifest what is *real, not what* seems *real!*

"Exactly," the fairies replied.

I was tiring of untangling the fairies' riddles. *What do you mean, 'exactly'?* I mentally communicated in a demanding tone. *Please use clear, plain terms with me.*

"Oh, thank you for telling us that! We don't know whether you're understanding us or not unless you tell us. Okay, you want plain English. That's what we'll now give you."

Good. If you speak to me in basic terms and I clearly understand the concepts for myself, it will make it easier for me to teach others.

"In addition to understanding the principles of manifestation, we want you to experience success with them. You just did some

major clearing and healing work concerning your romantic life. Your heart is now clean of residue from your past, so it is a blank slate upon which to sketch your desires. We'll work with you on manifesting a healed love life."

Oh, I would really appreciate that! It seems like I've had great success in all areas of my life except that one, I said.

"Then take detailed notes and follow these steps exactly," said the fairies. When I agreed, they began my lessons: "The first step of manifesting, as we said, is to have a blank slate in your heart, which you will use as your artist's canvas to create your new desires. You create a blank slate through the process of clearing and healing anything from your past that is related to your present desires.

"There are many ways to clear and heal, and you just experienced a very thorough and efficient one. Anyone can go by themselves to a natural location with wild plants, bushes, or trees and request help from the plant, bush, or tree people. Sit next to a plant, bush, or tree that attracts you, and have a mental conversation with the being who lives within that plant, bush, or tree. Ask for help from your heart, and you will never be denied this assistance. The plant, bush, or tree person will extract the related pain from your heart, mind, and body. As the tree explained to you, his energy amplified and brought your unhealed feelings to the surface.

"You will experience physical sensations during the clearing process, such as tingling, a feeling of air-pressure changes, and spasms of the muscles. They are strong but pleasant physical reactions to the releasement of old, negative emotions. When the clearing is complete, your body will be calm. You may even find yourself 'flattened' and temporarily unable to move. This is a good time to rest and contemplate your healing process."

That's exactly what I felt when the tree was helping me with my love-life issues, I recalled. And afterward, I really did feel that I was flat against the ground and unable to move.

It was a sense of great relief, very pleasant.

"The clearing process is nothing to fear. It is, however, a necessary component of manifestation.

"Once the heart has been purified and restored like a clean canvas, then we begin painting new images upon it. The second step of manifestation is this: coming to the realization that everything that you now have in your life—every relationship, situation, or possession—is there because of your expectation. Like a pregnant, expectant mother, you expected it all. The expectation is the conception that births the outcome."

So I've expected all the parts of my love life? What a horrible idea. But I instantly knew that it was true.

"It's largely because your heart was contaminated with old pain, like trying to paint an image upon a canvas that has five existing layers of old paintings upon it. The old images will bleed through and show up on the new painting. To have a clear new image, one needs to begin with a clean canvas. And you have created that by allowing the tree person to clear your heart of the old images of your love life."

What a relief! I exclaimed with gratitude. *I am so ready for a happy love life.*

"Exactly. That is step two of the manifestation process: ensuring that you are truly ready and feel deserving of your desire."

How can I be certain that I feel ready and deserving? I asked.

"It's readily apparent if you are not, through the process of trusting your inner teacher to guide you. Every being is aware of their inner teacher's guidance, but the only ones who trust and follow this guidance are those who are ready for their new desires to manifest. Those who don't feel ready or deserving always ignore or distrust their inner teacher."

Oh, I've certainly been in that position, and a lot of my clients and audience members have told me they've suffered from this, too.

"Every Earthly being has experienced moments of feeling unready or undeserving of new good coming into their lives. Otherwise, there would not be a need for any manifestation steps other than step one: clearing and healing the heart; step two: asking for what you desire; and step three: receiving it. An accepting heart can manifest anything continually. But, since most beings aren't ready to receive good without reservations, we offer additional steps."

I had my notebook and pen ready, poised to write down every detail of the fairies' secrets of manifestation.

"Much like you are doing right now, we ask that beings go into nature in seclusion with a journal and writing instrument. Sit next to a wild tree or bush, and close your eyes. Breathe for a while. Don't try to make anything happen."

Listening to My Heart

I followed the fairies' instructions precisely, positioning myself next to a eucalyptus tree and propping my back against its sturdy trunk. I then closed my eyes and breathed, seemingly in unison with the tree.

"Good. Now simply think of the topic of your desires. It could be anything: your career, your life purpose, your finances, health, moving to a new home, or—in your case—your love life. Again, don't try to control your thoughts or emotions. Simply allow your mind to focus upon the general topic. Continue to breathe in and out deeply, and focus upon your heart center.

"Ask your heart: What do YOU desire? Then, allow your heart's imagination to wander where it wants to go. Allow yourself to fantasize about what your heart craves and desires concerning whatever topic you have chosen to focus upon."

I placed my concentration on my heart, and I felt it swell

with warmth, like it was grateful for the attention. I mentally asked my heart, *What do you desire?* I repeated the question several times, until a strong idea and feeling overtook my attention. It was threatening at first, because it was such a sharp contrast to what I currently felt in my marriage. But I had to face my true feelings in order to heal my love life.

I knew that I desired—no, *craved*—a soulmate relationship with a spiritually minded man who would travel and give workshops with me. I wanted a partner in every sense of the word: romantically, spiritually, intellectually, and physically. I could feel, in my bones, what joy such a relationship would bring me.

"Do you feel ready for such a relationship?" the fairies whispered in my right ear.

I—I think so, I stammered.

"Step two of manifestation will occur when you can answer the question without reservation. Keep working on that, and we will then teach you step three."

❧ ❧ ❧

CHAPTER 10

The Angels of Abundance

My mind was practically blank as I walked home. I felt like everything I'd previously learned about relationships was topsy-turvy. How could I know so many facts and psychological theories and techniques with respect to relationships, yet not know the truths that the fairies were teaching me? I chastised myself for several more moments before I heard a familiar voice behind me.

"The point isn't to be perfect as a human, because you are already a perfect child of God."

It was the angels! I could always recognize the high frequency, love energy, and positive warmth of their comforting messages.

"As a human, the point is to be aware of your underlying intentions. As long as you intend to be loving, don't focus upon mistakes that you may make. When you make mistakes, give them to heaven."

What do you mean?

"Remember what the fairies taught you about the process of 'undoing.' Whenever you become aware that you have made a mistake, meaning an error in thinking based upon unloving or fearful thoughts, simply say, 'I admit that a mistake has been made, and I ask that all effects of these mistakes be undone in all directions of time for everyone concerned.'"

I repeated the affirmation in my mind and felt my body release regret and shame concerning my love life. I felt an inner sense of peace for the remainder of my walk home, partly from a drained feeling of releasing so much in one day. It was a satisfying feeling, but enervating nonetheless, as if I'd donated blood.

As I neared my home, I noticed Michael's car in the driveway. I tensed with some guilt, knowing that I hadn't communicated the extent of my unhappiness to him. We'd been so distant since my carjacking had catapulted me back on the spiritual path. He'd tolerated my changed attitude, my isolation during meditations, and my constant trips out of town to give workshops, so I didn't feel a need to upset him by making demands that he change into the spiritual soulmate I longed for. I reasoned that he couldn't help being skeptical about spirituality; it was who he was. After all, Michael had always told me that he had a private spirituality that he preferred not to discuss. Who was I to demand that he begin having deep philosophical discussions with me, just because that was what I craved?

I watched Michael work on the printing press in his home

office, where he created beautiful prints of nature scenery and sold them to art galleries. I told myself, *You're lucky to be with a man who makes his living creating beautiful artwork.* But my heart wasn't buying the line anymore. I had touched that part of my heart that is unabashedly honest, and I wasn't about to start covering up and lying at this point. I walked into my home office with the realization ringing in my mind like a fire alarm: *You're not happy in your marriage!*

I kept busy with some paperwork and pushed the thought out of my mind. But every time I'd have a free moment, the realization crept back in.

I lay down and closed my eyes, praying for help. I could feel my angels helping to calm my emotions. Once I reached a more peaceful and centered state, I recalled the haunting voice of the fairies asking me, *"Do you feel ready for such a relationship?"*

I asked myself, *Do I feel ready?*

The answer came to me immediately: As much as I wanted a great soulmate relationship, a part of me was frightened. I was afraid that Michael wasn't the man of my dreams, afraid of ending the relationship, afraid of starting over, afraid of what people might think if I got a divorce, and afraid of being alone. The fear of being alone had come up repeatedly as I reviewed my fears. I tuned in to my feelings and realized that—as painful as my current relationship was— there was an even greater pain associated with change.

I was worried about upsetting Michael if I admitted my unhappiness to him. I dreaded dealing with any defensiveness he might have, as if I were accusing him of being inadequate. I realized that I had *manifested* Michael, and had erred in not asking the Universe to provide me with a spiritually minded man. I had been so happy with Michael in the beginning, until the big spiritual wake-up call of the carjacking on July 15, 1995. After that, I'd found that I couldn't tell Michael about my thoughts and experiences because we didn't have a basis for a spiritual relationship.

Overwhelmed by my fears, I fell asleep. I dreamed that angels and fairies ran their fingers through my aura, lifting away little black snowflakes from it. The snowflakes and some dark-colored dust were in my aura like dandruff particles in hair. As the angels and fairies combed my aura, I felt very loved and peaceful.

The Archangel Michael's Messages

The dream was vivid, with intense colors and strong emotions. I saw myself sitting on a quartz granite rock, with angels and fairies surrounding me in a classroom-style seating arrangement. One large male angel, whom I recognized as Archangel Michael, was standing in front of the class.

He pointed a marker to a board that was unlike any chalkboard I'd seen in school before. Lightwaves emanated from his pointer, and information was transferred into my mind telepathically. Archangel Michael conveyed information about manifestation, and I understood his messages from the depth of my soul.

I awoke with a renewed sense of serenity, and an inner faith that told me that everything was going to be okay. I immediately reached for my nightstand journal and wrote down my memories of Archangel Michael's lessons on manifesting. I hurried to write everything before the essence of his message faded from my memory, and before my third-dimensional mind flattened his esoteric concepts. Here is what I wrote:

"There are beautiful sunrises and sunsets every day, and I don't need to do anything but notice them in order to enjoy them. If I don't go outside or look out the window, I miss the beautiful show of nature.

"In the same way, my inner sun is always creating beauty. My prayer is to notice and therefore enjoy this beauty in expression. I don't need to do anything else—it's not like a Santa Claus situation where I have to 'earn' the creations and manifestations of this Light. The Light shines joyfully and beautifully continuously, because that is its nature. My only role is to show up and notice the Light and its effects.

"I am now in the flow. I can see clearly how much my thoughts, feelings, and decisions influence the movie of my life. My awareness of Spirit means keeping a positive, pure, and loving focus; and this will shape positive, pure, and loving outcomes.

"It's as if Spirit is clay and my thoughts mold its outcome. If I consistently hold elevated, optimistic thoughts and feelings, I have a consistently happy and harmonious life. The angels also tune in to our true thoughts and feelings, and work behind-the-scenes to orchestrate the effects that our feelings and thoughts call forth.

"My Spirit is always attracting, magnetizing, and creating. My Spirit is love. Love always gives, provides, experiences, and expresses joy. Love is balanced in giving and receiving. Love wants for nothing; it is whole and wholly joyous. My Spirit is who I Am. Therefore, I am the process and the substance of abundance.

"My mind reflects or mirrors whatever it sees. If I look at (or focus upon) darkness, then I have a darkened mind. If I look at or focus upon light or love, then I have a light- and love-filled mind. It's my choice. I can look upon, or *notice, the abundance of good in the world, and have a mind that is filled with abundant thoughts of good.*

"Since what I think about is what I attract and create, then I definitely want only loving and abundant thoughts of good in my mind. What I focus upon and how I frame it (positive or negative) is like deciding what to feed my mind—junk food or healthful, life-sustaining food. I only want to see good so that my mind is filled with good, so that I create only good.

"Matter is illusion, and so is scarcity of any form. I can only experience scarcity if I choose that type of illusion. By choosing an abundant illusion, I'm not taking anything from anyone else. That would be impossible.

"In fact, when I allow myself to receive, I am in a better position to help others. Not only am I an inspiration to them, but I also have more energy, strength, and resources to give. So, it's not a matter of whether I deserve to receive—I do deserve to give. I therefore allow myself to receive good so that I may help others more effectively."

I reread what I wrote three times before its meaning sank in fully: I could manifest anything my heart desired, because my spirit was eternally creating. I laughed to myself at the realization: *I can't* not *manifest. I'm always manifesting! So I may as well manifest what I desire!*

I thought about all of the nights I spent in lonely hotel rooms while on the road. How desperately my heart longed for a soulmate relationship—to be with a man who would accompany me to my workshops because his heart was also centered upon being a spiritual teacher—a man who would be my friend, my spiritual companion, my lover, my true mate.

"So," the fairies' collective voice interrupted my thoughts, *"are you ready for the type of relationship that your heart desires?"*

Yes! I replied emphatically. *Yes, I am! In fact, I don't think I can keep up my current schedule of traveling and giving workshops unless I have my soulmate with me. I demand that the Universe produce a soulmate relationship for me. Unless he shows up, I quit!*

I wasn't acting-out a tantrum or being a prima donna. Rather, I was expressing long pent-up emotions of anger, frustration, and loneliness. I was absolutely crystal-clear in my new expectations: I deserved a spiritually minded mate who would travel with me. Maybe that would be Michael, maybe not. I just wanted my soulmate, whoever and wherever he was.

"*Very good,*" said the fairies. "*Very good. You have just completed the second step of manifesting by aligning your mind and heart, to feel what you desire, and also by knowing that you are ready for your desires to manifest and that you deserve them. Now, be ready to receive explicit instructions from your inner teacher, for the third step of manifesting is to be aware of, and to follow, this inner guidance.*"

Truth and Intimacy

It was nearly 4:30 in the afternoon by the time I reentered my office. I could hear Michael upstairs, cursing at his printer, which seemed to break down two or three times a week. I wondered if the angry words that I heard him utter were creating this experience for him. I also wondered if he would be open to learning the manifestation secrets that heaven was teaching me.

As we sat down for dinner, I broached the subject of my new book as a way of opening a conversation. I felt that we hadn't shared in a discussion about my work with the angels and the afterlife. Each time I brought up the subject, I felt that Michael and I engaged in a debate. I would tell him my feelings, and it seemed that he would play the role of devil's advocate or skeptic. My emotions would get so heated that I always ended each conversation by withdrawing.

However, I knew from my work as a psychotherapist that couples need emotional intimacy to survive—and emotional intimacy stemmed from discussing heartfelt topics with one another. How could I have emotional intimacy with Michael if I couldn't discuss the central topic of my personal and professional life?

After dinner, I retreated to my home office with a knot in my stomach and throat. I sat in front of my altar and closed my eyes. I asked my gut and throat, *What are you trying to tell me? Why are you tightened?* Then, I listened with my entire being, noticing what impressions arose in answer to my questions. I knew that the answers could come as feelings, thoughts, visions, an inner voice, or an overall impression.

A wave tightened over my body, followed by a release and ensuing relaxation. Then I had the realization, as my body revealed its truth to me: *I was afraid of how to change my relationship, and was uptight about orchestrating the change.* I gasped, realizing that I was trying to fix things without calling on my spiritual team for help.

I'm thinking that I have to do everything myself! I laughed. Here I was, an author and speaker who continually emphasized the importance of asking for help, and I'd forgotten my own advice. I knew, from prior experience, that the "how" of any Divinely guided life change is completely up to the infinite creative wisdom and love of the Maker.

Joyous Affirmations

"The key is to anchor your desires and expectations within your body," the fairies instructed. *"The method that we fairies use, with great success, is to joyously state our desires and expectations mentally or aloud while we move our body in nature. So, you could affirm your expectations while jogging, walking, stretching, or dancing outdoors."*

Each day during the coming week, I took the fairies' advice. During my runs and walks at the beach, I strongly affirmed, "I have a beautiful soulmate relationship! We travel and speak together! We live in a comfortable home near the ocean in Laguna Beach," and so on. Each day, I felt increasingly confident that my expectations were gestating.

Michael and I rarely spoke anymore; we were more like roommates. We didn't argue, but neither did we connect verbally or physically. Our dinners together were spent in front of the television set, and we'd go to our separate home offices after dinner. I wondered how and when I'd have the opportunity to speak with my husband about my heart's desires.

I prayed for help, and one evening, I turned off the television set and told Michael that we needed to talk. I explained to him that I was profoundly unhappy and was considering leaving him. He protested, but listened without becoming defensive. I said, "I realize that if I'm unhappy, you must be unhappy, too. When one partner is unhappy, both people in the couple are always affected."

He asked what he could do to help me feel happier. I was pleasantly relieved by his motivation to work with me. I felt hopeful about our marriage for the first time in years. I explained to him that I felt deeply lonely in the marriage, since he and I weren't communicating. "I would especially like to have discussions about spirituality," I said. "I don't need you to believe as I do, but I do need you to be *open* to my beliefs."

I also revealed how alone I felt while I was out on the road giving workshops. Michael explained that he was contained by his work, and that he couldn't leave without suffering financial consequences. I wondered aloud if there was any way for him to make money while on the road with me, and together, we realized that he could sell "goddess gowns"— long, flowing dresses—at my workshops.

Michael assembled a beautiful collection of gowns and began taking them to my workshops—no easy task, though, since his inventory required four huge suitcases. The cost of flying Michael to events, plus the hassle of dealing with heavy luggage, made his accompanying me an unpleasant and costly undertaking. After his fourth trip, we decided against future travels together.

I was back to going out on the road alone. Yes, my manager, Steve Allen, or my sons frequently accompanied me, but it wasn't the same as having a loving partner to snuggle with in my hotel room at night.

I still felt separate from Michael, unable to discuss my spiritual beliefs and experiences with him, without meeting a wall of silence or skepticism. One night, in my sterile hotel room, I put my foot down to the Universe: "Either you get me a soulmate relationship, or I quit!" I felt movement in my body as I spoke the words with 100 percent conviction.

❧ ❧ ❧

CHAPTER 11

Love and Laguna Yoga

My plane landed the next day at John Wayne airport. As I drove along Pacific Coast Highway to my home in Dana Point, I passed through Laguna Beach and had a sudden realization: "I belong in Laguna Beach!" I remembered how my Grandma Pearl had lived in Laguna Beach when I was a young adult. I loved the area—with its artist-colony feel and its flowers lining the seashore. As I drove along, I saw a clear vision of myself living in Laguna Beach near the ocean, feeling very peaceful and happy.

I put my suitcase in my office and found Michael so that I could announce my intention to him. "I need to live in Laguna Beach," I said matter-of-factly. Within two months, my vision came true. We moved to a quaint, geranium-clad cottage near the ocean in North Laguna. I loved jogging through exquisitely beautiful Heisler Park each morning, feeding the seagulls by day and watching the sunset each evening. My new level of happiness associated with this new locale carried me through my near-constant travels. Each time I was on the road, I hungrily missed Laguna Beach, like a lover yearning for her partner.

I also loved shopping at Laguna Beach's health-food grocery store, Wild Oats. One afternoon I looked at the notices posted on the Wild Oats bulletin board and saw a stack of calendars for yoga classes at a place called, "Laguna Yoga." I took one of the calendars, knowing that I was being Divinely guided.

Beginning Yoga

I intuitively felt that I was supposed to attend yoga classes, but I also felt intimidated. Sure, I was athletic, having engaged in cardiovascular activities such as jogging, in-line skating, and stair-climbing for many years, but I wasn't sure I was flexible enough for yoga. And how did people at yoga classes dress? I worried that I'd feel out of place. I procrastinated signing up for classes, but kept the schedule next to my telephone. Each time I saw the calendar, I felt a strong inner nudge: *"Go, go! Go to yoga!"*

Finally, I decided to do some research to help my comfort level. I stopped by Laguna Yoga one afternoon and looked at the clothing that everyone was wearing. I was relieved that the yoga students simply wore leggings and

T-shirts—clothes that I had an abundant supply of in my closet.

I purchased a three-month membership even before taking a trial class. I knew that it was important to make a commitment to yoga, even if I didn't enjoy it initially. I decided to take four beginner courses the first week, and I felt immediate results. The instructor, Annabel, reminded me of an incarnated fairy. She was sweet, supportive, and very inspiring. My feelings of relaxation and euphoria following each class amazed me. I also found that my psychic abilities were more heightened as a result of taking the class, as well as my ability to focus my thoughts. Yoga, I discovered, was a gift from God for those who have difficulty meditating.

After class, I heard several students talking about the owner of Laguna Yoga, a woman named Johnna. They spoke of her in warm terms, and I imagined that anyone who could create and run such a wonderful yoga center must be a sage. I looked forward to meeting her.

The next day I got my wish. All the students were sitting on yoga mats, awaiting the start of the class. The door to the studio opened, and several students excitedly said, "Hi, Johnna!" I looked at the 30-something young woman with the dark pixie haircut and big blue eyes and had an immediate knowingness: *Johnna and I are going to be really close friends.*

The next day, I brought Johnna a deck of my *Healing with the Angels Oracle Cards*. Three days later, I ran into her at Bank of America. She gave me a big hug and smile and told me how much she'd enjoyed the angel cards. "I pulled one before I walked into the bank just now!" she said enthusiastically.

Since this was my first opportunity to talk with Johnna privately, I asked about her work with Sai Baba, the Indian avatar. Johnna explained that she'd visited India the prior year and had attended many of Sai Baba's darshans, where he walked around the ashram and gave blessings to the many people gathered to see him. Johnna appealed to Sai Baba for a personal interview and was granted one. I was fascinated and impressed by Johnna, and glad to make a new friend. We made lunch plans.

Johnna and I soon became inseparable. I spent nearly every day at yoga class, and as my body and mind grew stronger, I made some important decisions. I saw that my marriage to Michael was not going to last. We'd tried marriage counseling, angel therapy, and prayer, but sometimes, healing looks different from what we expect. I felt very sure of the Divine guidance I'd received to leave the marriage, and I knew that this direction was in response to my prayers and manifestation work with the fairies.

When there was zero doubt in my mind, I approached Michael and asked him for a divorce for the second time in our marriage. The first time, 12 months earlier, he had asked me to give him another chance for an additional year. He had promised that things would be different during the coming months. I had honored that request, but at the end of the year, I was more unhappy in my marriage than ever. Without blaming anyone, I firmly asked him to leave. I felt no sadness—only tremendous relief.

A Magical Attraction

I continued attending yoga classes and felt my muscles growing stronger and more fluid. I was able to hold the various yoga asanas, or postures, with ease. Where in the past, the Downward Facing Dog asana—in which you are propped up on hands and feet, bent at the waist, with buttocks extended high into the sky—had been strenuous and painful, it now felt gloriously relaxing.

One evening I was in a class where we were doing a position that required us to lie on our backs and do twists. We'd put our hands out like a "T," and move our knees to the left and to the right. I bumped my right hand into the student next to me, and I looked over. My eyes met a man with shining blue eyes, silver hair, and a wide smile. My heart leapt, and I felt a strong attraction instantly. Throughout the class, the man and I exchanged smiles and bumped into each other accidentally. By the end of the class, I was smitten.

I *had* to talk with this man! At the end of the class, I discreetly followed him into the room where students put their shoes back on. "Hi, I'm Doreen," I introduced myself.

"Steven," he said, putting his hand into mine. There was something about his eyes and warm demeanor that made me feel comfortable. Steven introduced me to his daughter, Nicole, who worked at the front desk of Laguna Yoga.

The next day at lunch, Johnna and I discussed our love lives. She asked me, "Are there any guys at Laguna Yoga you're interested in? I'd be happy to intervene for you."

"As a matter of fact, there is one guy," I said. "His name is Steven; he's Nicole's father."

"Steven Farmer!" said Johnna. "Oh, he'd be perfect for you. He's a psychotherapist like you."

"Do you happen to know what his astrological sun sign is?" I asked.

"I'm pretty sure he's a Cancer," Johnna answered.

No wonder I had such instant chemistry with him! I thought. My father was a Cancer, and I tended to be attracted to Cancer men—although my relationships with them never seemed to last for long because the famous Cancer mood swings were difficult for me to take.

I had just read a powerful book on astrology that said that I, a Taurus born on April 29, would do best in a relationship with a Capricorn, but my interactions with these men had been frustrating. I'd met some extremely wonderful Capricorns who were romantically interested in me, but I'd never had any attraction toward *them*. My "chemical" reactions seemed to be limited to water-sign men, who, ultimately—as the astrology book confirmed—were not right for me.

"A Cancer. Oh, that's really interesting!" I said.

"Well, I'll talk to him and check it out for you," Johnna promised.

I couldn't get Steven out of my mind, and I checked with Johnna daily to see what she'd discovered. "I still haven't had a chance to talk with him," she said.

I bugged Johnna incessantly, inquiring about Steven. When I'd see Nicole, I'd send a "hello" to her father. I saw Steven at two more yoga classes, and then I didn't see him for some time. Johnna told me that, sadly, Steven's two brothers had passed away and that he was grief-stricken. I had an urge to call him to see if I could be of any assistance. After all, my spiritual and clinical work had taught me a lot about grief counseling. But something held me back from contacting him.

I accepted dates from other men, but I found the dating process painful and empty. I still longed for my Prince Charming who would be spiritually minded, health conscious, fun-loving, and with whom I would share a strong romantic and physical attraction. I even checked into dating services, but my soulmate seemed to elude me. I still hadn't forgotten about Steven Farmer, but each time I asked Johnna about him, she'd say something discouraging. It seemed that

I'd have to be content with my wonderful career and great health. Maybe we can't have it all, I decided. I should be satisfied with what I have.

But my peace of mind wavered, and one day I was on an airplane with my manager, Steve Allen. I complained bitterly to him about my romantic loneliness. Steve, a family man with a solid 25-year marriage and four small children, understood the importance of a loving home life. "Why don't you pull some of your angel cards and ask Archangel Michael about your love life?" he suggested.

I decided to take his advice. I pulled four cards from the *Healing with the Angels* oracle card deck. The cards were: "Soulmate," "New Love," "New Beginnings," and "Trust." I stared at the card spread. There was no doubt what it was telling me. I would meet my soulmate, and the New Beginnings card meant that the relationship would lead to marriage. The feeling of reassurance that came over me spread from my bones to my gut.

Steve took one look at the card spread and said, "See? I told you that everything's going to be okay." At that moment, I felt complete peace.

My workshops were taking me to many exciting places. I loved interacting with audience members and giving angel readings and signing books. I enjoyed the workshops, but the one-on-one interactions were what really fueled my heart and energy level.

However, I knew that my life was imbalanced, with so much travel and not enough rest or playtime. I also realized that Johnna was experiencing a similar form of burnout. "Let's go to Sedona for a time-out," I said to her one day.

We connected with Peter Sterling, a harpist who lives in Sedona. Peter and I had met six years earlier at a Whole Life Expo. I'd been mesmerized by his music, and immediately bought his CD, *Harp Magic*. I played it while channeling the majority of *Angel Therapy*, and I credited the frequencies of his angelic music with helping me to be a clear channel.

Since that time, Peter, who has a clairaudient connection with the angelic and fairy realms, has played the harp at several of my workshops. He and Johnna were acquainted, and we were all happy to get together for a holiday in Sedona.

❦ ❦ ❦

CHAPTER 12

The Fairies and Leprechauns of Sedona

The red monolith mountain peaks of Sedona had never looked so beautiful, contrasted with the shocking blue Arizona sky. Johnna and I jogged along a red dirt trail that was absolutely quiet except for our pounding shoes. We stopped along the road and panted, each meditating quietly.

I was lonely in my love life, and my faith in finding my soulmate was shaky. However, I continued to affirm my expectations about being in a spiritually rich relationship. My trust in the angels' continual promises that *"he's coming, he's coming,"* was buoyed by the strong energy of the Sedona vortexes. It had been a disappointing year, love-wise, but I hadn't given up hope. Something inside me told me that "he"—that elusive man the angels spoke about, and whom I could feel in my heart—was just around the corner.

Peter, Johnna, and I drove to an area in Oak Creek Canyon, a part of Sedona known to the locals as "The Fairy Pools." We waded in the ice-cold stream, refreshing our sun-drenched bodies. I could see and feel thousands of fairies and leprechauns in the glens surrounding the stream. They welcomed Peter, Johnna, and I enthusiastically, and let me know that they had information for my forthcoming book, *Healing with the Fairies.*

Messages at Mushroom Rock

Peter said to me, "Before you arrived, I was here at the fairy pools. The fairies told me that they wanted you to spend time with them on 'Mushroom Rock.'" Peter then led me to a giant, flat rock jutting out of a wide stream. He and Johnna went hiking, leaving me alone with the elementals who resided on and near Mushroom Rock.

I lay down on my back upon the rock, holding two crys-tal stones I had purchased at the "Angels, Art, and Crystals" shop in Sedona. One, a heart-shaped sugalite nugget, I placed upon my neck. Sugalite always opened my verbal expression and channeling facilities. The feeling I received when wearing or holding sugalite was nearly identical to the emotions I experienced when I spoke with Archangel Michael. The second stone was a quartz crystal point that I placed upon my third eye, to further open my channel of clairvoyance.

Almost immediately, I fell into a semi-trance, like a dream

state with awareness. In my mind's eye, I could see several powerful leprechauns standing over me, each measuring two to three feet high. I also saw fairies flying acrobatically over me, swimming through the air like fish in an aquarium.

The leprechauns seemed to switch on a mental movie in my mind. I saw the mushrooms in my Dana Point home's backyard. *"Do you remember these?"* they asked me pointedly.

Yes, of course.

"Those mushrooms were our homes! You mowed them down!"

I didn't do it. My ex-husband Michael did! I protested.

"You sanctioned the action by standing by idly and doing nothing. How would you like someone to destroy your home?"

I wept hot, stinging tears of guilt and grief.

"Each time, we'd forgive you and regrow a new mushroom home. You were working so closely with the fairies at that time that we thought you'd see the connection! After all, you invited us into your lives. Yet, when we arrived and set up a home in your backyard, what did you do? You destroyed our home each time!"

By now, I was devastated and pleaded with them for forgiveness.

"It's the same way with our home, the planet Earth. The human race has no idea how much they are destroying the natural resources. You must begin teaching more pointedly the importance—no, the urgency—of living in harmony with nature. Please urge your audience members to forsake pesticides in their foods so that crops won't be sprayed with so many poisons. Please tell them to recycle, and to take care of our Earth."

I will. I promise!

Then, exhausted from my tears, I lay panting on Mushroom Rock. I realized that I was completely alone, from a human standpoint. Johnna and Peter were gone, and I couldn't hear any cars or other signs of human contact. I pulled my arms around me to ward off feelings of vulnerability.

I hadn't allowed myself to be completely alone in some time. Sure, I'd been by myself in hotel rooms or at home, but I'd always had the option of connecting with others by telephone, e-mail, or a personal visit. However, at this moment, there was no immediate way of contacting another human. It was just the elements, the elementals, and me.

A Deep Cleansing

As I lay there, I came to understand that I'd stayed in my marriage much longer than I desired due to this fear of being alone. I then felt the comforting and familiar feeling of being covered with the fairies. *They're extracting and healing the painful and negative residue from my marriage and divorce!* I realized with joy and gratitude.

The fairies gathered the negative thought-forms, like workers picking apples from a tree. As before, when the fairies had worked on me, my body felt paralyzed as I observed the process from a semi-trance state. It was nearly sunset before they completed their clearing work, and I fell asleep with blessed relief, feeling that I'd been freed from the old pain.

Peter and Johnna woke me gently upon their return from the hike.

❀ ❀ ❀

CHAPTER 13

The Reality of Mythical Creatures

Most Friday nights found me giving psychic readings to my workshop audience members. I enjoyed being on the road meeting new people, and I especially liked giving readings. For one thing, I learned a great deal from each one. The angels and deceased loved ones always taught me a lot about life and death.

I also discovered that many people have elementals as their spirit guides or guardian angels. For instance, those who are incarnated elementals often have several fairies flitting over their shoulders, and people whose life purpose involves helping the environment, animals, or plants always have elementals hovering around them.

One time I was doing an angel reading for a young college student. She'd asked who was with her in the spirit world, so I was in a semi-trance, scanning her head and shoulders to identify her guides and angels. She had an assortment of deceased relatives with her, whom we identified as her mother, her maternal grandmother, and a paternal uncle. She was profoundly grateful to be able to speak with her mother, and was radiating a blissful smile. I then tuned in to see who else was with her, when suddenly, I gasped, "Oh my gosh! You have a unicorn next to you!"

The unicorn was whitish-blue, almost opalescent in color. It was small, maybe three feet tall from hoof to ear tip. And there, in the middle of its forelock, sprouted a magical horn. This was no deceased pony hanging around its former owner, like most pets do after they pass on. No, this was a genuine unicorn!

I asked her, "Do you like unicorns?"

"Oh yes, very much!" she exclaimed.

I received a clairsentient (through my feelings) message signaling that the unicorn was with her due to her affection for the species. In the same way that people who love angels usually have lots of guardian angels in their vicinity, this is also true for those who love unicorns. I've seen unicorns around dozens of other people since then. While they aren't as commonly seen as angels or fairies, unicorns are definitely real, existing on a higher dimension.

I started to discover that many of the so-called mythical creatures really do exist. They are on an energy plane that is higher-vibrating than our physical dimension, so our eyes usually don't detect these beings. I wondered, were unicorns a species that once walked upon the earth, but were then wiped out and became extinct—and are now only to be found in the spirit world? I thought of the many Renaissance paintings I'd seen that portrayed unicorns as real, physical animals. Perhaps artists in centuries past were more clairvoyantly attuned than we are.

Thought-forms of Fear

Through giving thousands of readings, I came to realize that leprechauns, dragons, and gnomes also exist in the spirit world. I found that beings who have bird, butterfly, or dragonfly wings are creations of Divine light, who can be trusted to be helpful and benevolent souls. The beings with batlike wings and talons, however, are usually creations of the ego, and are therefore devoid of an inner light. They are bringers of chaos, depression, and anxiety.

Some myths call these batlike beings the "protectors," but my research has repeatedly shown me that they inspire pain and havoc, not protection. They often clasp their talons into the shoulder blades of people who unwittingly invite them in, by owning statues of gargoyles. These people will find that they have excruciating shoulder pain, caused by the talons and the dark energy of the bat-winged creatures.

Whenever I see a client with a gargoyle on their shoulders, I immediately call Archangel Michael to escort the being away. In all cases, these "gargoyle-ectomies" have been successful, unless my client was hanging on to the darkness that the bat-winged creature brought with it. My clients reported immediate relief from shoulder and neck pain following these sessions, and I began teaching the method to chiropractors and physical therapists at my training sessions. The feedback I received from these professionals was very encouraging. However, I continually emphasized to audience members that we can self-heal by calling upon Archangel Michael or any of our other friends in the spirit world.

Meeting a Mermaid

One day I was sitting on the beach in Laguna in the middle of a meditation. My eyes were open as I gazed upon the ocean. I watched the sea sprites dance in and out of the water—opalescent little fairies guarding the water and its inhabitants. Suddenly I saw a large etheric being jump out of the water like a flying dolphin. I watched with my mouth open, realizing that I had just seen a mermaid!

My work with the elemental kingdom had definitely made me open-minded, but even I had a hard time accepting the reality of a mermaid. I decided that I had imagined it. Probably, I had simply seen a pelican diving for a fish and had mistaken the bird for a mermaid. But there she was again, hovering above the water. She wasn't a physical being, but an etheric, translucent image that I saw simultaneously in my mind's eye and also with my physical eyes.

She was spectacularly gorgeous, perhaps the most beautiful woman I had ever seen. The turquoise lower-half of her body shimmered with sequin scales. Her hair cascaded like tumbles of flaxen. And she had angel wings! Two enormous, feathery white wings met her shoulder blades.

We looked at each other momentarily, and I felt my heart jump toward her in an embrace of sisterly familiarity. She conveyed to me a universal love, for both the ocean and for humanity. Intuitively, I heard her say, *"I am one of many mermaids on the dense part of the astral plane. We work fervently behind-the-scenes, helping humans to make better choices for the treatment of our ocean and our future. Many beings* (she clairvoyantly showed me images of fish and other under-water creatures) *depend upon our waters' health. You see, the ocean is a living, breathing entity, and her creations depend entirely upon her health. Please, you humans, ensure the health of Mother Earth, our entire planet, and in many ways, our solar system, by ceasing your polluting ways."*

I felt a deep kinship with the mermaid, as I've always felt drawn to the ocean. She seemed to be a wonderful blend of the elemental and angelic kingdoms. I asked about her wings, since I hadn't recalled seeing images of mermaids with angel wings.

"Mermaids, as you have imagined us, really do exist. I am from a branch of that tribe called the Mer-Angels. We are the equivalent of you lightworkers—beings on special assignment to help with the changing energy of the world. Our cousins are the Mer-Fairies— they are smaller mermaids with fairy wings that look like dragon-fly or butterfly wings.

"We Mer-Angels are like the archangels of the ocean, and the Mer-Fairies oversee the lakes, rivers, streams, and ponds. Together, the Mer-Angels and Mer-Fairies guard the bodies of water and their inhabitants. These waterbodies are like the blood and other fluids within the human body. It is essential that they do not experience any further pollution. At this point, the water bodies are nearly at their limit."

What can we do to help? I asked earnestly.

"Many of you are recycling, and that definitely helps! It's vital that you make the switch to low-polluting cleaning supplies, such as the detergents available at health-food stores. Please use organic products more often. The run-off from commercial cleaning supplies and pesticides threatens many of the water species, and will ulti-mately affect all life on the planet and neighboring solar systems.

"Now is the time to take control of the water environment! The incarnated elementals have life purposes to help us clean up

the environment. And we Mer-Angels have complete faith that the lightworkers and incarnated elementals will do their job. We trust that they will educate the humans about recycling, using low-polluting cleaning supplies, eating organic food, and taking personal responsibility for the environment. We are counting on their help!"

I promised the Mer-Angel that I would deliver her message in the pages of a book, as well as to any incarnated elementals with whom I worked. She again emphasized how important each individual lightworker and incarnated elemental is to the overall health of the earth. *"Each person can help us enormously!"* she added. With that, her etheric body turned to mist, like the spray of the surf. Then she was gone.

The Call of the Dolphins

I breathed deeply, still taking in the Mer-Angel's message and loving energy. As I looked out to the swells of water where she had hovered, I saw the happily familiar sight of fins moving in unison. *Dolphins!* I said to myself. *The dolphins are here!*

I watched the pod of dolphins leap and dance as they maintained their group focus of traveling south toward San Diego. Each time I saw the dolphins, their magical grace mesmerized me. Today, following my conversation with the Mer-Angel, I felt newly awakened sensations of love for the Divine creatures of the sea. I thought how lovely it would be to swim with the dolphins . . . someday.

I stopped by the Wild Oats health-food store later in the day, keeping my promise to the Mer-Angel to use only low-polluting cleaning supplies. I had been recycling and eating a primarily organic diet for several years, but my cleaning cabinet hadn't reflected my conviction to environmental causes. That day, I brought my life further into integrity by purchasing environmentally sound dishwashing and laundry detergent, as well as shampoo, conditioner, and bar soap. I also bought paper towels and toilet paper made with recycled, unbleached paper. They cost a bit more than the brands at conventional grocery stores, but I knew I was making an investment in the environment with my purchases. I also felt a boost in my self-esteem, something I'd always noticed whenever I did the right thing.

At the checkstand, I scanned the various magazines for sale. One, called *Magical Blend,* caught my eye. I hadn't read the magazine in years, but that particular issue seemed to call my name.

When I got home, I checked my mail and noticed an envelope from my father. He regularly sent me clippings of articles he thought I'd find interesting. Today, I was pleasantly surprised that he'd sent me an article about a woman who swam with the dolphins. I had placed "swimming with dolphins" on my mental list of things to do someday. I'd talked with several people who had experienced such swims, including my mother, and my friends Arielle Ford and Bonnie Coleen. All three had told me about the transformative effect that the dolphins had had upon them.

Arielle described the love she saw in "her" dolphin's eyes as completely unconditional, like one reads about with near-death experiencers who are healed by the Light and their spirit guides. My mother said she'd never experienced such joy, and her photo of being with a dolphin showed the widest smile on her face that I'd ever seen. My friend Bonnie Coleen took frequent trips to Kona, Hawaii, because she found her experiences with the dolphins to be rejuvenating and refreshing.

I walked into my bedroom with the copy of *Magical Blend* magazine I'd just bought. A page opened up to a long article about swimming with the dolphins. *That's three times in one day that I've had a message about swimming with the dolphins,* I noted to myself.

The next day, I went on my computer to check my e-mail. I'd forgotten about the dolphins until I opened a letter from someone asking if I had swum with the dolphins. *What's going on?* I wondered.

Two weeks later, I had a breakfast meeting scheduled with a friend at "The Cottage" restaurant near my home in North Laguna Beach. As we waited to be seated, I glanced over at the other patrons. A man was reading the *Los Angeles Times,* and I saw a huge color photograph on the page he had open. It was blue, and looked strangely like a picture of dolphins. *It can't be,* I mused. I turned to look straight at the newspaper, and sure enough, he was reading a travel section with a headline describing "Swimming with the Dolphins."

Since the moment I'd bought *Magical Blend,* I had received two or three messages daily related to dolphin encounters. By now, I was sure that the dolphins were calling me to join them. I was emotionally ready to go, but unsure how I was to create a dolphin encounter. I contacted my friends who had been with the dolphins, but my gut told me that my encounter would happen in a different way.

Since I'd been well trained by the angelic realm to surrender any worries about how to put my guidance into action, I didn't stress out about what steps to take. I knew that I'd be led. Even if I didn't *initially* notice or believe the guidance, I trusted that I'd *eventually* notice and believe it. That's why I received so many simultaneous messages to swim with the dolphins—Divine guidance always comes repetitively, until we finally "get it."

My guidance told me, *"Just commit to swimming with the dolphins. Put it out there, and tell other people about your intentions. It will come together on its own very quickly."*

A couple of days later, I was scheduled to give a midweek evening lecture at the Tustin Unity Church. During the talk, I discussed the characteristics of true Divine guidance. I mentioned my messages about dolphin encounters as an example of how Divine guidance is repetitive.

I said to the audience, "I know I'm being called to have a dolphin encounter because of this repetitive guidance. I have let go of 'how' it will happen, and I am just following the steps that are given to me."

Following the lecture, a man in attendance named Glenn Jaffrey approached me. I had met Glenn earlier in the year when I lectured with Jimmy Twyman in Joshua Tree, California, over Easter weekend. Jimmy, author of *Emissary of Light* (and Gregg Braden, author of *Awakening to Zero Point*), and I had conducted several global prayers in which people around the world simultaneously visualized peace for five minutes. Glenn had introduced himself to me as a long-time student of metaphysics, and as a travel agent who specialized in tours to Hawaii.

"Were you serious about wanting to go swim with the dolphins?" he asked me.

"Oh, yes." I replied. "I know for a fact that the dolphins are calling me to join them. I know that I will eventually swim with them, even if I'm not sure how it will happen."

"I'll call you tomorrow," said Glenn. I noticed an impish look in his eye, and I wondered if he was an incarnated leprechaun.

❦ ❦ ❦

CHAPTER 14

"Believe in Us!"

The next morning, I slipped on my jogging shoes and ran through Heisler Park, heading to Main Beach for my morning run. I loved the feeling of pounding upon the sand and breathing the fresh salt air. I ran to the quartz rocks near Sleepy Hollow Drive and sat down to meditate.

Immediately, the fairies came to me. *"We're glad that you're going to visit the dolphins,"* they said. *"They have some very important information for you, and some energy to add to your lightwork."*

I wasn't exactly sure what the fairies meant, but I trusted that I'd know soon enough. At this point, I had taken my hands completely off the steering wheel, so to speak. I'd surrendered control to God and heaven, trusting that—like air traffic controllers—they had a bird's-eye view of my life's purpose and my future.

I am happy to be working with you and the elemental kingdom, I said to the fairies. I felt gratitude in my heart for their contributions to the environment. My own life had taken on a magical sense of new doors opening since I'd begun working with them. I felt their fingerprints on many of the happy synchronicities in my life.

The Truth about Fairies

"Many people mistakenly believe that we're mischievous," the fairies said, *"but you've found us to be good friends, haven't you?"*

Yes, and I do trust you, I replied.

"We are often misperceived because we're compared to the angels. It's an unfair comparison, though, because our life work keeps us in the densest energy fields of the earth. The angels are egoless. Just like all creations are perfect beings of Divine light in truth, the angels see this truth. They don't focus on the surface personalities or illusions of problems. This is their way of spiritually healing—by focusing upon and drawing out the inner perfection to rise to the surface.

"But we fairies and other elementals are in the thick of the illusion. We see humans thoughtlessly throwing trash upon nature, and polluting with pesticides and toxins. It's difficult for us to warm up to humans unless we see a sincere desire and understanding on their part to help us. However, when we find a human, lightworker, or incarnated elemental who sincerely desires to help the environment, our hearts are gladdened.

"We need humans in more ways than one. Not only do we need

their help in cleaning the environment, but we also need their help in believing in us. Please help us, Doreen, to let people know that we fairies and elementals are real.

"Please tell people to believe in us! Believe in us! People's belief in us gives us power and energy, which enables us to be more productive. The more people believe in us, the more power we have. We believe that all of us can be friends and work together toward our common goals."

I'm happy to do whatever I can to teach about your reality and your mission, I said. *And I do want to thank you for all that you've taught me, and the new sense of playfulness and happiness you've brought into my life. I am truly happy, and so grateful for all that I have. When I find my soulmate, I will have the life of my dreams.*

"We will help you with that endeavor, Doreen. You will soon meet your soulmate. We promise."

Yes, I can feel the truth of that. I know that he will soon be in my life, I concurred.

When I returned home, I picked up a message on my answering machine from Glenn Jaffrey, the metaphysical travel agent. "You really are meant to go swim with the dolphins, Doreen," he said cryptically. "Please call me."

When I reached him on the phone, Glenn explained that the Hilton Waikoloa Hotel in Kona, Hawaii, was interested in having me hold a seminar at their facilities. They wanted me to be their guest and experience their dolphin encounter program—free of charge. I was ecstatic! It felt like the dolphins and the elementals had orchestrated the trip for me, and had paid for it to boot. We settled on a date in late October.

That evening, I decided to take the 6:30 "Restorative" yoga class with Annabel at Laguna Yoga. It was one of my favorite classes, both because I enjoyed Annabel's sweet style of teaching, and also because she had us hold the yoga poses for extended periods of time. We'd put a yoga strap around our feet to support our asanas, and really stretch the muscles thoroughly, but gently. All of the poses in the Restorative class felt wonderful, and I always left there feeling refreshed. Unfortunately, because it was held on Friday nights when I was usually giving a workshop somewhere, I rarely got to attend the class.

Reconnecting with Steven

I walked into the reception area to sign in for the class, and several of my friends greeted me. As I was talking with Sue, a psychotherapist friend of mine, I heard a male voice behind her say, "Hi, Doreen!" I looked up and glanced at the man addressing me. "It's me, Steven Farmer. Remember me?"

Of course I remembered him. For a year I'd thought about him, but each time I asked Johnna about him, I'd felt rejected. It seemed as if Johnna was asking him out on my behalf, and that he was turning her (me) down, so I just smiled at him and went back to my conversation with Sue. During the class, I didn't give Steven a second glance, since I'd written him off months earlier as being "chronically disinterested in me."

The yoga class was wonderful, and I left feeling euphoric. Two days later, I stopped into the yoga studio to drop off some decks of my *Healing with the Angels Oracle Cards*, which Johnna sold at her shop. Nicole Farmer was behind the desk, and she gave me a big smile and hug. Nicole and I had gotten to know each other over the past year, and I genuinely liked her.

She and I seemed to have similar outlooks on a lot of life

issues, including dating and men. As I was getting ready to leave, Nicole remarked, "My dad said something about you after the yoga class last week."

I stopped and turned to face her. Nicole was incredibly lovely, with delicate porcelain skin, baby blue eyes, and naturally blonde hair. She looked just like a beautiful, opalescent, incarnated fairy. I could even see her translucent dragonfly wings beating behind her shoulder blades.

Nicole continued, "My dad said, 'I never realized that Doreen was so attractive.'"

I looked at Nicole and felt a strong wave of happiness. I wrote my home and cell phone numbers on a paper, and handed it to her. "Then please tell your dad to call me and ask me out," I said with a smile.

"I will," she said.

I didn't put much energy into thinking about Steven Farmer, due to not hearing from him or seeing him throughout the year. Besides, I was busy creating a new deck of oracle cards called *Healing with the Fairies*. The fairies were busily instructing me about which words to write in the guidebook accompanying the cards.

So when I received a message on my machine from Steven a few days later, I was actually surprised—pleasantly so. His message asked me to join him for breakfast, brunch, or a mid-morning coffee and a beach walk on Sunday. My choice. However, I knew that I'd probably be too nervous to eat, and I also don't drink coffee, so I called him back and made a date to meet him for a bottle of water and a beach walk.

I woke up Sunday morning feeling as anxious as a schoolgirl going on her first date. My nervousness resulted in my being ten minutes late for our agreed-upon meeting at Deidrich's Coffee on Pacific Coast Highway. First, I had to figure out what to wear. Through prayer, I felt guided to select a denim skirt and beige tank top, with a swimsuit underneath in case we decided to swim at the beach. Second, I had to contend with Sunday-morning traffic. And third, the only parking space I could find was three blocks from Deidrich's.

By the time I walked into the coffee shop, I was a nervous wreck. I breathed deeply to center myself, looking around for Steven. He was nowhere within the coffee shop, so I walked outside. I worried, *What if I don't remember what he looks like?* After all, I really hadn't looked at him closely in nearly a year.

But my fears were unfounded. As I stepped outside onto Deidrich's patio, a man called out, "Doreen!" There sat a stunningly handsome silver-haired man waving to me. Could that be Steven? He sported a "Laguna Yoga" T-shirt, and stood up to hug me hello. I felt both comforted and flustered.

Steven asked if I wanted anything to drink or eat before going on our beach walk. I declined, since my throat felt tight with anticipation, and I didn't know if I could eat or drink. I'd learned that each astrological sign has an "Achilles heel" somewhere in their bodies, and as a Taurus, mine was the throat. This area revealed my unexpressed emotions, and, while I almost never got sick, I'd lose my voice now and then. At that moment, standing next to the awesome Steven Farmer, I felt quiet and content.

We walked across the street to Main Beach and began walking south along the surf. Steven began telling me about himself: He held a master's degree in counseling psychology.

"Me, too!" I said. "Where did you get your degree?"

"At Chapman University."

"Me, too!" I said again.

Steven told me that he'd written several books about child abuse, including the best-selling work, *Adult Children of Abusive Parents*. I explained that my clinical specialty had been eating disorders, particularly for those who had a history of child abuse. My doctoral dissertation had been on the link between child abuse and eating disorders, which had turned into my first Hay House book, *Losing Your Pounds of Pain*. We also discovered that we both had two of the same publishers, CompCare and Lowell House.

He asked what books I was currently writing. I told him that I was in the midst of two books—one being the very book you now read, and the other a more mainstream book, *The Care and Feeding of Indigo Children*.

Would it scare Steven if I told him that I was writing a book about fairies? I decided to tell him the truth. After all, I was looking for a man who accepted my spiritual pursuits.

"You believe in fairies?" he asked.

Oops, I thought, *he's judging me.*

Steven continued, "I just attended a workshop about Celtic devas and fairies on Friday. I think that it's so neat that you're writing about them."

Wow!

Then Steven told me about his studies in shamanism. His beliefs in life-after-death mirrored and complemented my own so much that I felt like I was floating. "What's your sun sign?" he asked me.

"I'm a Taurus."

"Oh, my darlin'!" he exclaimed, putting his strong arm around my shoulders. "I've always been told that I should be with a Taurus lady."

"What sign are you?"

"I'm a Capricorn." Now I was in shock. All the astrologers and astrology books had recommended that I should be with a Capricorn man. Their advice had always frustrated me because I'd never felt a chemical attraction toward any

Capricorns. But I was completely attracted to Steven, and the more he talked, the more I felt myself melting in response to his words.

"I thought Johnna told me you were a Cancer sign," I remarked, as we sat on a granite rock near the Surf and Sand Hotel.

"Nope, I'm a Capricorn, with Taurus rising," he stated.

"Amazing," I replied. "I'm a Taurus, with Capricorn rising." We walked in comfortable silence for a few paces, and then continued sharing personal information with each other. Steven told me how his two daughters, Nicole, 20, and Catherine, 18, had lived with him for the past several years. His relationship with them reminded me of my own experiences with my sons, Chuck, 22, and Grant, 20. I had been friends with Steven's daughter, Nicole, for the past year, and my sons had gotten to know and like her, too. Steven and I seemed to have so much in common!

But I was still bothered by the nagging question of why Steven had taken a year to ask me out on a date. However, it became clear when he told me about the turmoil in his life over the past 12 months: His two brothers had passed away within one month of each other, right after we had met in yoga class. Then, a few months later, he closed a retail business that he had run for several years. "I didn't feel emotionally ready for a relationship until just recently," he said.

We walked back toward the beach in front of Heisler Park and found an inviting spot to rest. The sun was warm and glowing, and the waves looked so appealing. "Want to go for a swim?" I asked Steven.

We jumped and played in the surf like two kids, side-by-side. I felt too shy to touch Steven, and he kept his distance from me, too. But inside, my heart was opening to him in a new and wondrous way.

Steven and I returned to our spot on the sand to dry off in the warm afternoon sun. He opened his waist pack and pulled out some papers. "I want to read you some things," he said. Steven then began reading me beautiful poetry! His voice was strong and expressive, and he'd stop occasionally to look me in the eyes before continuing his recitation.

When we parted later in the day, we hugged warmly. The next day, I went to Los Angeles to meet with television producers who were interested in creating a show with me as the host. My sons went with me, and we had fun discussing show ideas with the producers. We returned to Orange County feeling positive about the meeting.

I walked into my condominium and checked my answering machine. "I don't know if you've had a chance to read your e-mail yet," said a deep male voice, "but I was wondering if you'd go to the movies with me tonight." It was Steven, asking me out! What a perfect way to end a glorious day.

🌸 🌸 🌸

CHAPTER 15

A Romantic Reunion

It was a warm and lovely evening, and we drove with the convertible top down to a movie theater in Aliso Viejo. We were on our way to see *Almost Famous*, a movie about rock-and-roll that I'd wanted to see.

I realized that, although I knew about Steven's present work as a spiritual psychotherapist and author, I didn't know much about his upbringing.

"So, where were you born and raised?" I asked.

"I was born in Cedar Rapids, Iowa, in 1948."

Steven was ten years older than I was. *Perfect*, I thought. I tended to be attracted to men in that age range.

He continued, "Then, in 1960, our family moved to North Hollywood, California."

"You're kidding!" I said. "In 1960, *my* family moved to North Hollywood."

"Amazing!" he said. "Whereabouts did you live?"

I replied, "Near Victory and Vineland."

"Hmm, that's just about the area where I lived."

I continued, "I lived on a little cul-de-sac called Craner Avenue."

Steven looked at me and exclaimed in amazement, "Wait a minute! *Our* family lived on Craner Avenue!"

My mind reeled and my heart leapt as I realized who he was. "You're the guy! You're the guy!" I was practically yelling.

"What?"

"You're the guy who lived at the end of the block in the apartments on Craner Avenue! You're Steven, the guy I had my first crush on! I used to stare at you, but you never seemed to notice me—I guess because I was so much younger than you." Since I hadn't seen Steven in more than 30 years, I'd had no idea up till now that he was the boy-next-door from my childhood days.

Luckily, we had just pulled into the movie theater's parking lot, because I doubt that Steven or I could have coherently driven the car any longer. We were both in shock.

"Are you sure?" he asked.

I then described details about Craner Avenue that distinguished it from other streets. We compared notes on our neighbors, who included the talent agent of Jay North (a.k.a. Dennis the Menace), and a man who collected drag race cars. We were clearly talking about the same street and the same time frame.

I was reunited with my very first crush! How romantic

that I'd experienced love-at-first-sight with the same guy—twice in one lifetime! The movie was a blur to both of us. We didn't even touch our popcorn, but instead, held each other close throughout the entire two hours.

After the movie, we drove back to Laguna Beach, still wondering what all of this meant. Steven and I obviously had much in common, and were deeply attracted to one another on many levels. And now this mystical twist in which we discovered that he was the boy-next-door! I felt the hand of the angels, fairies, and our deceased loved ones playing a part in our reunion.

Evidence of Heaven's Help

Steven and I spoke of how the angels must have laughed just before we realized we'd known each other as kids. He said, "I can just imagine everyone in heaven saying, 'Okay, Steven and Doreen are just about to find out about their common childhood history!' and all of them enjoying our shock at learning this news."

As we stood to say good-night, Steven held me tight. Then we kissed, shyly at first, exploring, building, warming. Our lips touched with the emotion of tentative questions, until they were answered with expressions of joy, shared revelations, and passion.

The next day, I received a phone call from a woman named Jessica. "I got your name and number from Cherie Allen," she said. "There's a group of us in Laguna Beach who do work with fairies and mermaids. I'm a sculptor, and the others in the group include authors like yourself, painters, and people who make fairy-related things. We're getting together for a brunch at my house on Saturday. We'd love for you to join us."

I knew that I belonged at that group meeting. Saturday night would be my third date with Steven, and I had offered to make him dinner at my place. I knew I'd be nervous, since we hadn't seen each other in a week. Steven had been teaching a workshop in Santa Fe, and we were limited to phone calls and e-mails.

"Sure, I'd love to come to the group," I told Jessica. Then I asked her, "Do you know Katherine Kiss, who is known as the fairy queen?"

"No, who is she?"

"Katherine has a booth every summer and winter at the Sawdust Festival here in Laguna. She makes incredibly beautiful fairy dolls. I have two myself. She's opening a store dedicated to fairies in Laguna Beach called 'Through Fairy Halls.' You must meet her."

"Great," said Jessica. "Please invite her for me. Can't wait to meet both of you!"

I searched through my papers for Katherine Kiss's phone number and couldn't find it anywhere. *Please help me find her number,* I mentally implored the fairies as I reached for my car keys to leave for the store.

On the way to Wild Oats, I saw a tall blonde woman in a long dress standing on the side of a Pacific Coast Highway restaurant. I stared in disbelief— it was Katherine Kiss! I was so excited by the fairies' instant manifestation that I pulled my car to the side of the road and enthusiastically called out, "Katherine! Katherine!"

I told her how I'd just asked the fairies to connect us. Since Katherine and I had never run into each other in town before, we agreed that the fairies had definitely orchestrated our rendezvous. I discussed the upcoming fairy group meeting, and she agreed to attend. She also gave me her phone number, since I'd apparently misplaced it.

I thanked the fairies as I drove away from Katherine. As I turned onto Mermaid Street, I saw another familiar figure. *My goodness!* I said to the fairies. *You are really trying to convince me of something here,* as I slowed down to say hello to Cherie Allen, the woman who had told Jessica to invite me to the fairy group.

The first time I saw Cherie, she was walking down Second Avenue. I saw her from a distance and remarked to a friend of mine, "Look, there goes an incarnated mermaid."

My friend looked startled and asked, "How did you know?"

"Know what?"

"That everyone calls Cherie 'The Mermaid Lady.'"

"I didn't know that, but I did immediately notice that she looks just like a mermaid! She's got that Mae West look to her, with big ocean-colored eyes, cascading thick blonde hair, and she's dressed in a body-skimming turquoise gown."

"Well, Cherie draws paintings of mermaids."

"Really? Well, I must talk with her," I said.

I ran into Cherie about two weeks later at Wild Oats. We had a brief, but delightful, discussion, where she showed me her products sold at Wild Oats, including her mermaid-themed greeting cards and her ceramic mermaid incense holders. I showed her my *Healing with the Angels Oracle Cards,* which Wild Oats sold in their health-and-beauty section. We exchanged phone numbers, promising to meet for lunch in the near future.

But I really hadn't made time to get to know Cherie, except for running into her at the store frequently. As I pulled up to her on this day, I thought of the synchronicity of seeing her moments after Jessica had called me about the fairy group meeting, and after running into Katherine Kiss.

Cherie and I hugged, and I told her about the fairies' doings that morning.

On the following Saturday morning, I stopped at Wild Oats market to shop for food for that evening's dinner with Steven. I brought the groceries to Jessica's house, since our group meeting would end about one hour before Steven was set to arrive at my home. I worried whether I'd have time to cook, shower, and get changed for my date, so I surrendered all my cares to God, the fairies, and the angels.

Jessica greeted me at the door, dressed in a pink ball gown, looking just like an Earth fairy. She waved a sparkly wand over my head and handed me a bright pink concoction in a champagne glass. "It's non-alcoholic," she said. "The fairies will make us naturally high today!"

Her house was decorated with the fairy sculptures she had made. "I have to show you this mermaid sculpture that I made with Cherie as the model." Jessica escorted me to a corner by her oceanview window. I gasped as I looked at the lifelike rendering of Cherie, complete with a spiraling mermaid tail.

Katherine Kiss, Cherie Allen, and several other fairy lovers, artists, writers, and doll makers were there, and the first meeting of "The Laguna Beach Fairy and Mermaid Society" was officially in motion. We had a great time, engaging in a show-and-tell with each other's fairy products. I had the preliminary color proofs of my new card deck, *Healing with the Fairies Oracle Cards,* with me. The group gave it their hearty approval.

Twin Flames

I left the meeting feeling that I'd joined a new sisterhood, and my mood was buoyant but somewhat nervous as I drove home to get ready for my third date with Steven. He arrived right on time—a good sign, I thought.

We hugged warmly, and then he said, "I think we both know where this is going, and I just want to get everything out in the open. I brought a list of all my bad characteristics so you can know what you're getting into." I laughed with joy at Steven's openness and expressiveness. How refreshing he was!

Steven's list of "bad" traits seemed mild and normal, almost complementary to my own negative traits. "We all have shadows," Steven said. "It's just important to be aware of them and not them rule you." I couldn't have agreed more.

When he was done reading his list, I said, "That's all? Where are the bad parts?" He chuckled and gave me a big hug.

Then I shared my own list of shadows with him. Steven didn't run away. In fact, he sat closer to me when I was done. He looked at me with sparkling eyes, and I thought, *Oh, we're falling in love!* I didn't fight the thought or the emotion, feeling very safe with Steven, like I'd known him a million years.

We shared a beautiful evening together. The next day, I went to the beach and sat on a quartz rock to meditate and talk with the fairies. *I know that you were behind my reconnection with Steven,* I said to them, *and I just want to thank you.*

Intuitively, the fairies let me know that they *had* helped orchestrate many of the synchronicities surrounding our meeting. However, we also had help from many others in heaven, including Steven's deceased mother and brothers; my Grandma Pearl; the Archangel Michael; and our guardian angels. "Thank you all!" I said, with gratitude and joy filling my heart. The fairies confirmed that Steven and I had shared many lifetimes together.

Within two weeks, Steven and I were inseparable. We continued to learn about our commonalities, and the message was clear: We were more than soulmates. We were "twin flames," a term given to people who are from the same soul, and who separate into distinctly male and female personas. Sometimes, twin flames don't incarnate together. It was common for one to be in a body, and the other to act as a spirit guide.

We learned from the "I Am" teachings of the ascended masters that when twin flames incarnate together, it often signals their final incarnation on Earth. It's an opportunity for both partners to form an Earthly union to create one final "hurrah" while in their last life here.

Steven and I had both spent our lifetimes working toward purposeful, meaningful aims. We were both passionate lightworkers, committed to helping usher in a new age of peace. We were both givers and helpers, personally and professionally. In our prior relationships, we'd experienced imbalances of being the "giver" who was matched with a "taker." These sorts of relationships can be draining for the giver, and it can make the taker feel guilty. "Two givers in a relationship is ideal," Steven said to me, "and that's what you and I have."

We discovered that there had been many instances in our lives when we could have met. Starting from childhood, we could have become friends and begun a lifetime relationship. Then, in 1988, when we were both with CompCare publishers, we could have met. Or, when we both lived on the Newport Beach peninsula in 1993 and were both single, we could have had a relationship blossom. Or, we could have met as students of Chapman University. The list of our life intersections went on and on.

Apparently, soulmates are brought together continually, until the couple finally connects. At first, Steven and I grieved over our lifetime apart. "We could have avoided so much pain in our other relationships if only we'd gotten together earlier in our lives!" we'd say to each other. But ultimately, we decided that the timing just hadn't been right previously. We both needed to grow and learn from other relationships.

Hawaiian Manifestations

My trip to Hawaii to swim with the dolphins was scheduled for October 20. One night I thought, *I wonder if Steven could come with me!* When I asked him, Steven said he would love to accompany me, but wasn't sure if he could get away on such short notice. His schedule was as busy as my own. Not only did he have a private psychotherapy practice, but he also ran group therapy sessions at a recovery program, and taught classes at Saddleback Community College.

It took two days for Steven to rearrange his schedule, and I prayed with bated breath the entire time. In my mind, I could see Steven in Kona with me. I knew from prior experiences that, whenever I could clearly see something, it always came about. Steven *had* to come play with the dolphins with me. It was just too perfect to pass up!

I was eating lunch in Hollywood with my manager, Steve Allen; my son, Chuck; and a great friend, Dorian Hannaway. Dorian was a high-powered television producer who had taken Steve Allen and me under her skillful and loving wing. She was instrumental during the meetings we'd had lately, in which Hollywood bigwigs were considering a television talk show for me.

Since I'd previously hosted a mid-afternoon radio show in Nashville, as well as several cable TV programs, I knew that such a venture would be a huge time and work commitment. I had surrendered the process to God, knowing that if He wanted me to perform service in that way, it would happen. If it wasn't meant to be, I wasn't entirely attached to the idea. Our meetings had indicated that I probably would soon have my own show. That day was no exception.

As we ate lunch at Wolfgang Puck's, I expressed my gratitude to everyone at the table for their participation, support, and love. I was so fortunate to be surrounded by great people who believed in angels, and who regularly consulted with heaven for guidance—so different from the stereotypical Hollywood personas who were simply interested in ego gratification! And yet, every time I was involved with the media, I found that there were hundreds of spiritually minded people working in the industry. I'd made dozens of television appearances concerning angels, and had been on hundreds of radio shows. In almost all cases, the producers and hosts would share their mystical stories with me. Both Hollywood and New York were filled with believers in miracles, and many entertainment professionals felt that bringing such stories to the airwaves was part of their Divine mission.

Just then, my cell phone rang. *How Hollywood,* I thought. It was my friend Jimmy Twyman, my peace-prayer partner.

"I'm going to Jerusalem to conduct a peace-prayer concert," he told me. Jimmy, who is known as the "Peace Troubadour," has set prayers from the 12 major religions to music. He plays guitar and sings the prayers in countries all over the globe, especially those places experiencing strife or war. Jimmy had played in Croatia, Bosnia, Ireland, and other locations.

"We need to hold a global prayer vigil for the Middle East while I'm there," he said.

I asked when he was going to Jerusalem.

"On the 19th of October," Jimmy replied.

"Amazing," I said. "I'm going to be swimming with the dolphins in Kona on October 21. The dolphins called me to be with them, and maybe this is the reason why. I know that their energy will anchor and amplify the power of our prayers. Can we hold the peace prayer on that day?"

"The 21st would be perfect for me, too!" Jimmy agreed. "I'll call Gregg [Braden], and we'll get everything in motion."

I hung up and shared the good news with Steve Allen, Dorian, and Chuck. They all agreed that the timing of the dolphin encounter and prayer vigil was Divine. The next morning, I received more good news: Steven had successfully rearranged his schedule, allowing him to join me in Kona. I shrieked like a contest winner at the news! I just knew that our trip would be exceptionally powerful and pleasurable.

❦ ❦ ❦

CHAPTER 16

The Call of the Dolphins

"I have never had such an enjoyable flight," I said to Steven as our plane touched down. We had laughed, hugged, and written on our respective laptop computers during the flight.

The big island of Hawaii was lushly dressed in thick green palm trees, and the weather was a perfect 82 degrees.

Our home base for the next week would be the Hilton Waikoloa Hotel in Kona. As we strolled the grounds, Steven and I walked arm-in-arm like honeymooners, and he stopped to pick a plumeria flower from a fragrant tree. He looked me in the eye and placed the flower behind my left ear, "This shows that you're taken," he said with a loving smile. I felt so loved—and in such a healthy way—by Steven.

We went to our room, and Steven pulled out his acoustic Martin guitar. "I want to sing you something," he said. Steven proceeded to sing a beautifully poetic love song. If I wasn't already wooed by his romantic charms, his song opened my heart further.

Steven finished the song, then he pulled me closer for a romantic kiss. As he held me, I saw an image in front of me of an impish pixielike person with hooves and a flute. It was Pan, the famous flute-playing half-goat, half-boy! I hadn't thought about Pan since I'd read about him in elementary school, yet his image was so clear. Pan stared at me wordlessly, then he was gone, and I returned to the awareness of Steven's embrace.

Steven and I were set to have three different dolphin encounters on our trip. The first would be at the hotel in the enclosed lagoon with domesticated dolphins. I was unsure of the ethics of being with captive dolphins, but I trusted my gut instinct, which told me to go ahead and experience being with the dolphins at the Hilton.

Besides, Glenn Jaffrey had booked guaranteed encounters for Steven and me. Normally, hotel guests had to put their name in a lottery drawing, hoping that they would be among the 30 people selected each day to swim with the dolphins. Since Steven and I were fortunate enough to be confirmed dolphin swimmers, we felt grateful, and looked forward to it immensely.

Our second and third dolphin encounters would be out in the wild. Before we'd left on the trip, I prayed for guidance with respect to swimming with the dolphins. I was guided to explore the Internet, where I happened upon a woman named Nancy Sweatt who conducted wild dolphin encounters. Nancy was a metaphysical student and long-time follower of Louise Hay's work. I felt chills as I talked with her by phone, validating that I'd contacted the right person.

I learned about the controversies surrounding dolphin encounters. The two schools of thought had to do with swimming with wild dolphins versus swimming with contained dolphins. One group believes that humans frighten and disrupt the dolphins in the wild. The second argues that contained dolphins are kept from their natural environment. Both sides seemed to present valid points, so I decided to check out the situation for myself.

Like Touching an Angel

Steven and I walked to the Hilton's dolphin lagoon with anticipation. We'd looked forward to this day from the moment Steven confirmed he could join me in Hawaii. The Dolphin Quest staff was warm and friendly. As we waded into the lagoon, they signaled for a dolphin to come to us. A big, beautiful female dolphin named "Malaya" would be our dolphin friend throughout the encounter.

First, the instructor asked us to put our hand on Malaya's underbelly and feel her heart beating. I looked her in the eye and saw an expression of loving contentment beaming back at me. I felt like I was touching an angel. *This dolphin isn't in any pain,* I immediately thought.

I then received an intuitive reply from Malaya: *"We are well treated, and although we miss our home in the ocean, we are on a mission to open the hearts of humans—not only to us dolphins, but so that love can permeate their lives. In this situation, we are able to affect many humans' lives deeply. Please don't have one moment of pity for us, for we are truly happy. We are able to rise above any material anguish and see the bigger picture."*

The instructor worked with Steven, Malaya, and me. We were able to kiss, hug, and play with her for nearly two hours. At the end of that time, I felt like I was floating on a cushion of magical energy. Steven was blissed-out as well. We slept like babies that evening.

Prayer and Surrender

The next morning, October 21, was the day scheduled for the peace prayer for the Middle East. Jimmy, Gregg, and I spoke via teleconferencing, which was broadcast on the **worldpuja.org** Website. The Webmaster was able to confirm that people from all around the world were joining our peace prayer.

"Prayer is so much more powerful than any bombs or guns," Jimmy said, speaking from a telephone in Jerusalem. Gregg agreed, and talked about the importance of aligning our emotions with our thoughts during the peace prayer. He pointed out that our feelings were the catalyst for any manifestation process.

Immediately after the peace prayer, Steven and I drove to Jack's Diving Locker in Kona, where we met Nancy Sweatt. She had clear blue eyes and sun-bleached hair, and her softly padded body reminded me of a dolphin. Her necklace, sarong, and hat all carried images of dolphins. I could tell that dolphins were the center of her life.

Nancy escorted us to a small motorboat called "The Blue Dolphin," captained by a young Hawaiian man named Kawika. We motored out into the harbor, and right away we saw a pod of dolphins. Kawika stopped the boat, and we all jumped into the water, but the dolphins disappeared.

We then saw them dancing and jumping in another area. Nancy said that if we would just wait patiently, the dolphins would come back. But I wasn't feeling patient—I really wanted to swim with them, so I asked if we could take the boat out to where they were. Nancy agreed, so we steered the boat over to that area. We dove in, and again, the dolphins disappeared.

I was starting to feel a little frustrated, so as I was swimming, I began praying and meditating. I decided to surrender the entire situation and let go of trying to be in control. At that exact moment, Kawika yelled excitedly, "There are the dolphins—right there!" The lesson was that I needed to stop chasing them and simply let the situation be.

Once I relaxed and let go, the dolphins seemed to instantly appear in our presence. They were underneath us, and Nancy, Steven, and I swam side-by-side like a human pod, right next to the dolphin pod! As I swam, there was a tube of dancing white sparkles of light that seemed to glow from above and shine right down into the water. I felt like I was looking into the tunnel of light described by near-death experiencers.

Dolphin Communications

Swimming above the dolphins was incredible, like running alongside a herd of wild antelope. Suddenly, one dolphin swam off by himself to the right. I followed him, and lost all track of Nancy and Steven. I seemed to be swimming extremely fast, nearing the dolphin. He cocked his head to the left to look at me, and my heart melted. I began cooing a spontaneous sound of joy, like a happy baby. I felt that he heard me, because he kept looking at me.

I had never swum so fast in my life! Soon, I felt tired, and I mentally asked the dolphin to stop and wait for me. At that instant, he stopped swimming. I caught up to him, and we began swimming side-by-side. There was a sense of cama- raderie and playfulness in this connection with him. He swam up ahead of me, and I again asked him to stop and wait for me to catch up. The moment I had this thought, his tail instantly ceased all movement. *Okay, so I'm not imagining it; he really does hear my thoughts,* I concluded with amazement.

I briefly wondered if I should look for Steven and Nancy, but then realized that this moment had opened itself up for a reason. I began laughing uncontrollably, like I would do if I were on an amusement park ride. But this was no ride. This was a meeting with an incredible creature, who was truly connecting with me out in the wild.

After the swim, I was euphoric as Nancy, Steven, Kawika, and I motored along in the boat. We spotted another pod of dolphins, and once again, we dove into the water. But once we were in the water, we couldn't find the dolphins. I could "feel" that they were to our left, and suddenly they appeared on the water's surface, to our left. *Okay,* I thought, *I can trust that my intuition really is connecting me with these magnificent beings.*

We swam toward the pod but couldn't find them. Kawika, sitting on the boat, kept pointing to where he saw the dolphins appearing, but as soon as we'd swim to that area, they were nowhere in sight. Finally, Nancy and I caught up to a large family of dolphins. They swam deep below us in murky water, and we could only see them like shadows. Then they disappeared.

Swimming by myself, I intuitively received the message from the dolphins: *"Don't focus on swimming with our bodies;*

that is a separation thought of Us and Them. See us, know us, and feel us as one with you. Incorporate our energy into your heart. Anyone can connect with us, our energy, and our messages, by doing this."

Steven and I climbed back into the boat. We cuddled on a padded bench with a large beach towel covering us to shield us from the wind as the boat motored back to the harbor. I told him about my experiences with the dolphins, and he shared with me that he'd also had some revealing insights during his encounters with these magnificent creatures.

"Yesterday," he said, "while we were with the dolphins at the Hilton, I was intrigued by one of the dolphin's scars. And remember how you didn't even notice those scars at all?"

I nodded.

"And today," Steven continued, "one particular dolphin captured my attention, and I found myself swimming alone with him. I noted that one of his back dorsal fins looked like it had been partially chewed off. It was interesting to me that in both of my dolphin encounters, I was shown the wounds of the animals. This makes sense, since in my writing and psychotherapy practice, healing wounds is a good part of my work.

"This particular dolphin with the damaged fin communicated to me while we were swimming. He said, *'I was wounded by a boat propeller. Yet in spite of the fact that humans are imposing themselves into our domain, we know that it is absolutely necessary that we continue to welcome you humans into our home so that we can teach and guide you.'"*

A few hours later, I was on the sofa in our hotel room. Steven sang a hauntingly beautiful song while playing his guitar. I felt a sadness in my heart—not from the song, but from missing the dolphins. I realized that, just like a near-death experiencer, I had touched so much beauty and love while swimming with them that I wanted more.

I was so happy to realize that I'd be with the dolphins the very next morning. I told Steven that I felt like crying, knowing that I'd miss them when I returned home. He said, "Being in the ocean with the dolphins was like floating in heaven with the angels, and there's a part of you—like in everyone—that remembers being back home in heaven. The dolphins are reminding you of the angels back home, and floating weightlessly in the water reminds you of having no body and being free in heaven."

I kissed him with gratitude for his comforting words and wise heart. That night, we openly discussed some of the fears we had about our relationship. After all, Steven and I were continually getting closer emotionally. This process normally brings up fears of being hurt, and other "shadow" or negative feelings. By discussing these fears openly, Steven and I helped each other feel safe enough to further open our hearts to each other. We were even able to laugh at some of our fears, realizing how unfounded they were once they were exposed through discussion.

We awoke the next morning, excited to rejoin Nancy and the dolphins for another day of encounters. This time, Nancy brought a friend of hers, a spiritual counselor named Carol. Carol explained that she taught art therapy courses and frequently worked with the fairy realm, personally and professionally.

I was excited to connect with Carol, who exuded a warm, relaxed energy. We discussed our experiences with the fairies and elementals. Then Carol said, "Just the other night, I had an experience with Pan in my art class."

"Pan?" I asked. "Please tell me more." How interesting, considering I hadn't thought about Pan in 30 years, yet I'd clearly seen him the other night while kissing Steven. And now Carol mentioned him out-of-the-blue.

"I was teaching a painting class, and I saw Pan jumping into—of all things—my *pans* of paint. He made quite a mess, literally. But I know that he didn't mean any harm. He was trying to get our attention."

"Did you find out what his message was?"

"I felt like he was urging us to play, let go, and have fun, especially during creative pursuits," Carol replied.

I knew that Carol's message was a sign that I needed to talk with Pan. I made a mental note to communicate with him as soon as possible.

The Importance of Playing

As we motored along, we saw many pods of dolphins. They seemed to enjoy swimming beside our boat. Several dolphins jumped mightily into the air, thrusting their aero-dynamic bodies into spins and twirls before rebounding below the blue water.

Steven studied them. "I think they're playing just for the joy of it," he said.

Then he asked Nancy for confirmation: "Are they jumping out of the water like that for a specific purpose, or for the sheer pleasure of it?"

Nancy smiled and said, "The dolphins know the purpose of playfulness. They spin and jump for joy, even though it probably slows down their route of travel. The dolphins have definitely taught me the importance of playing."

Steven and I looked at each other and winked. Since we'd been together, we had incorporated a lot of playfulness into our daily schedules. He tickled me lightly, and I giggled. Then we hugged.

We watched, fascinated by the wisdom of these great creatures. They were true lightworkers, giving to the world by helping us humans rediscover our inner children, our telepathic natures. Most important, they were also helping us open our hearts. They didn't have any pretenses or worries about their clothing, housing, or food. All of their needs were provided for them, as a beautiful example of, "Seek ye first the kingdom of God, and everything else shall be added unto you."

"Would you like to visit Queen's Bath?" Nancy asked us. "It's a magical place that's loaded with fairies."

Intrigued, Steven and I eagerly agreed.

Captain Drew motored his boat to a white, sandy beach that was surrounded by acres of lava rocks. "This beach is totally secluded. You can't walk or drive to it," he said. "The only way to get to Queen's Bath is by boat." The beach reminded me of tropical island posters, the kind you see at travel agencies. The water was shockingly translucent, like turquoise cellophane. Lazy palm trees slumped over sugary white sand, backdropped by an endlessly blue sky—creating an atmosphere of complete relaxation.

Captain Drew dropped anchor a few yards off-shore, and everyone jumped in the ocean to swim to the beach. I was surprised by how buoyant I was, and I concluded that this water was particularly salty. My fins and snorkel helped me navigate underwater effortlessly, and I felt like a mermaid who was truly in her element.

I caught sight of Steven, who motioned for me to join him. He pointed beneath the surface and smiled at me as I noticed a huge sea turtle skimming the shallow ocean floor. Steven and I both dove to accompany the great turtle, each of us gently petting the fellow once in order to make a tactile connection with him.

We swam along with the turtle beneath the sea, in a truly magical moment. Steven reached for my hand, and we swam hand-in-hand. It was like flying through the heavens together. Then we bid good-bye to our friend the turtle and headed toward shore. Captain Drew, Nancy, and Carol let us know that they intended to give Steven and me some privacy, and we didn't argue.

Steven and I walked together to the area of the beach that held the Queen's Bath: Behind a sand dune, a large freshwater pond was covered with reeds around its outer edges. Nancy had told us earlier, "The pond looks just like a cervix and womb," and she was right! The shape of the reeds and the pond looked like an anatomically correct drawing of the female reproductive system.

Steven and I were mesmerized as we waded into the shallow pond. The icy water met our feet with an initial resistance, then gave way to our gentle treading as we walked toward the "womb."

"Let's do a baptismal ceremony on ourselves," I suggested. Steven readily agreed, and we took turns sprinkling handfuls of fresh water upon each other.

"This is to release all toxins from our past," I said. He smiled and breathed deeply, then exhaled with gusto.

"And this is a symbol of the purity of our love," he said, sprinkling water over my head and shoulders. The spray cooled my sun-drenched shoulders. Steven and I embraced in a kiss usually reserved for wedding ceremonies. What joy we'd found in each other's companionship and embrace! I thanked the fairies aloud for their help in reuniting Steven and me.

Playing with Shadows

Just then, we heard loud giggles. Was it the fairies? We looked up and saw two children pointing at us. Their father seemed to scold the children, asking them to leave us alone. Momentarily embarrassed at being discovered during a tender moment, Steven and I felt compelled to leave.

Then I remembered my earlier discussion with Carol. I had told Steven about seeing Pan during our kiss the previous evening, and also about Carol's comments about him. "Let's see if we can contact him for a message before we leave the Queen's Bath," I said to Steven.

We both closed our eyes and mentally asked Pan for his words. I clearly heard a male voice say in my right ear: *"Play with your shadows. Face them with the spirit of fun and playfulness."*

I relayed this message to Steven, and he said, "That's amazingly similar to what I heard. I received a message that we shouldn't be afraid of our nakedness; that we go into the world unadorned, unwilling to be ashamed or embarrassed of who we *truly* are, including our shadows."

Both Steven and I had heard the same advice from Pan. We had learned about the importance of playfulness from the dolphins, and now Pan was validating what we'd already experienced in our relationship: openly admitting our "character flaws" to each other and ourselves. Steven and I had already experienced the relief and release that happened when we laughed at our idiosyncrasies, neuroses, and dark sides. Instead of hiding or feeling ashamed of our ego natures, we had exposed them to the healing light—in the spirit of laughter.

❧ ❧ ❧

CHAPTER 17

Declarations of Love

During the weeks and months following our trip to Kona, Steven and I grew increasingly close and fell even more deeply in love. I was enthralled at being in a love relationship where I could openly discuss my conversations with the angels and fairies. Steven and I often spoke to Archangel Michael together, and we also participated in spiritual ceremonies and meditations.

We'd frequently say to each other, "I never knew that love could be so wonderful!" He began accompanying me to workshops, and often co-led seminars. I was no longer lonely while traveling, and I renewed my commitment to giving workshops worldwide.

We consecrated our union in a spiritual ceremony presided over by a shamanic teacher named Jade Wah'oo. It was a beautiful ritual in which Steven and I professed our commitment to spending our life together and told one another about the depth of our love. Jade blessed our union with smoke from cedar, sweetgrass, sage, and powerful prayers.

My relationship with the elemental kingdom grew deeper, too. The more I worked with the fairies, the more I saw the magical beauty they brought to our lives.

Transported by Love

On a Friday afternoon in early December, Steven and I drove his truck to John Wayne Airport. We were scheduled to take a flight to San Francisco so I could give a speech that evening in Palo Alto. We were just getting ready to board our United Airlines plane when a gate agent announced that a Delta jet had just landed on the airport's only runway and had blown three tires. It was a miracle that the plane hadn't crash-landed.

However, the jet was stuck on the runway, and no other planes could depart or land at the airport. But I had to get to San Francisco! I was scheduled to talk in front of several hundred people at 7:30 that evening!

Steven and I prayed, turning the situation over to heaven. We asked a few other people connected with that evening's seminar to pray, also. The prayers were palpable, and I believe they created the solution by giving me Divine guidance. Steven and I received very strong impressions that we shouldn't wait for John Wayne to reopen. Instead, we should fly out of another airport.

We checked for the next available Bay Area flight with any airline, from any Southern California airport. The only flight that would get me to San Francisco in time for my event was leaving in 90 minutes out of Los Angeles International Airport (LAX). Could Steven and I get to LAX in less than an hour, in Friday evening's rush-hour traffic? Normally it was an hour's drive, even in light traffic.

Only a miracle would get us there in time for the flight. And then we remembered that the truck was out of gas. We'd planned to refuel it on our drive home from the airport when we returned from the Bay Area. However, now we'd be forced to stop for gas when we were already running late.

I asked the fairies and Archangel Michael to help us. Then I recalled what my son Chuck had taught me about time-warping. After all, Chuck frequently drove me to the airport when we were running late. He'd explain, "Don't look at the clock at all. Don't think about where you are, relative to the location you're trying to get to. Only think about one thing: what time you need to be at your destination. Let go of all other thoughts, and hold faith that you'll get there on time. Somehow the Universe shifts and allows you to manifest getting there on time."

To get my mind off of time concerns, I engaged Steven in a deep and interesting conversation. I asked him questions such as, "What was your favorite Christmas present when you were a child?" We ended up talking nonstop, all the way to LAX. I felt completely relaxed, assured that we'd make our flight—even though it seemed like an illogical goal, considering the circumstances. Yet, along the way, the carpool lane was absolutely free and clear, with no traffic jams. We easily arrived at LAX in under 40 minutes.

Going Home Again

The next day, we took a return flight to Los Angeles, since we'd left Steven's truck in the LAX parking lot. While we were in the air, I turned to Steven and said, "You know what would be really fun to do since it's Saturday and there isn't much traffic today? How about driving to our childhood neighborhood in North Hollywood?"

Steven grinned and readily agreed. "It's only a half hour from the airport," he said.

I hadn't been to the neighborhood since I was 10 years old, and Steven hadn't been there since he was 16. As we turned right onto Craner Avenue, I felt like I'd traveled into a time tunnel. Nothing had changed!

As we pulled up in front of my childhood home, I felt like I was in a daze, realizing that even the landscaping hadn't been altered in the last 30 years. Steven and I climbed out of his truck, walking arm-in-arm.

The situation started to feel even more surreal when I realized that both of us felt equal amounts of shock upon seeing our old neighborhood. I had been with other people who had revisited their childhood homes, but I was always able to remain detached and supportive because I wasn't directly involved. But on this occasion, both Steven and I were on the same wavelength—dealing with a real déjà-vu scenario.

I stared at my family's former home, the place where I'd first consciously had clairvoyant experiences. I looked at the hedge on our neighbor's lawn where I'd once seen a man crouching—but when I'd told my friends about the man, they couldn't see him. The hedge reminded me of the pain I'd suffered because my clairvoyance had made me feel different from other people.

Steven listened empathetically as I brought up my

childhood memories. On the one hand, I was raised in a loving and empowering family system—imagine having parents who encouraged the use of affirmations, visualization, and prayer to heal and manifest. Yet, in spite of all these advantages, I suffered because of my sensitivity to other children's tauntings ("You're weird!"), and my parents' lack of acknowledgment of my clairvoyance.

Steven embraced me tightly and said, "Everything's okay now. I'm here, and I love you *so* deeply." He looked me in the eyes, ensuring that I truly heard his words, and I felt the depth of his profound love.

We walked to his apartment building, and I watched Steven's breath deepen and his eyes drift far away. He was remembering, reliving, a time long ago. Since I had spent my childhood playing at his apartment complex with my girlfriend Stephanie, I joined in the memories.

There was the mosaic pathway that I recalled playing on! It sure had shrunk in size since I was a child. And there was the grassy mound where my mind held the frozen memory of Steven standing so many years earlier.

"Sweetheart," I asked, "can you stand right here?" Since Steven knew about my memory, he readily agreed. He stood in the exact same position that I had envisioned, looking away from me toward the pool. My breath quickened at the sight—so familiar, but with both of us taller and older. Then I approached him from behind until I walked around to face him. Steven pulled me close and warmly kissed me.

I felt my breathing change radically so that it extended deep into my belly. I hadn't realized how shallow my breath was until that moment. Steven's affection opened my heart, like Prince Charming's kiss awakening Sleeping Beauty. I felt a glacier melt that had surrounded my heart since it had felt rebuffed by Steven—my very first love—so many years ago. My early experience of unrequited love had set the tone for my entire love life, and I knew the pattern was now healed. Steven was my first, and my last, love.

Resolutions of Romance

"Look at this!" Steven held up a typewritten page for me to see. "These are the New Year's resolutions that I made one year ago." It was New Year's Eve, and we were preparing to lead a midnight meditation at Laguna Yoga.

Steven showed me how he'd outlined, in complete detail, his intentions for the year. Nearly every one of them had come true, in undreamed-of ways. His major intention for a relationship sounded like a detailed account of the union that he and I had formed. He wrote, in present-tense affirmation style, his desire to manifest a woman who was in her early 40s, who was highly creative, who was on the spiritual path, and so on. He described that the relationship would be with "my twin flame, my one true love, the one I'll spend the rest of my life with." As I read the description, I realized that Steven had manifested me!

That evening at the meditation, Steven and I sat on folded yoga mats gazing at the altar that Glenn Jaffrey, the spiritual travel agent, had arranged for us. It held various incense holders, essential oils, and feathers to wave over smoldering sage. I had brought candles with me in the colors representing each major chakra.

Steven and I led the audience through a deep chakra-clearing ceremony as I lit each candle, corresponding to the topics we were clearing. For instance, as we cleared away fears about, or resistance to, money, I lit the red candle, symbolizing the root chakra.

We then led the attendees through a meditation that I had recorded on my audio program *Manifesting with the Angels*. The "progression" allowed audience members to see one year into the future, if they followed their Divine guidance. We then anchored the meditation by focusing on feeling grateful for the gifts that Spirit would give us throughout the coming year.

Steven led the group through a movement ceremony, in which he asked everyone to stand and move intuitively to a musical recording. I found myself letting go of inhibitions, joyfully bending and swaying to the music. The dim lighting and blissful energy in the room seemed to give us all permission to dance with freedom, without constraint.

It was nearly midnight, so we resumed our lotus positions on the yoga mats. I realized that Steven and I were sitting two feet from the exact place where we had been reintroduced in yoga class one year earlier.

We asked the audience members to join us in a free-form chanting ceremony to usher in the New Year. We all began chanting, "Ohm," the tone that symbolizes the Creation, and which engenders the power of manifestation. We didn't worry if we were saying the Ohm's in unison or not, and very soon, the room was filled with waves of Ohm's. The natural rhythm of all of us saying "Ohm" at various times sounded like a beautiful symphony.

Steven and I were holding hands during the chanting. The clock struck midnight, and 20 seconds later, Steven squeezed my hand tightly. We were all chanting with our eyes closed, but his hand-squeeze brought me back to awareness. I opened my eyes and looked at Steven. He was looking at me with his eyes intensely open.

As I stared into his ocean-blue eyes, Steven looked at me and said, "Will you marry me?"

I blinked with disbelief, since my consciousness was so altered by the chanting ceremony. "Are you serious?" I asked.

Steven smiled lovingly. "Oh, yes. Very serious. Would you marry me?"

"Yes," I replied. "Of course, I'll marry you. I've loved you my whole life, Steven."

"So you just said yes?" Steven asked, to confirm my answer.

"Yes, I would love to marry you!" I exclaimed.

Steven leaned over and kissed me. The other people in the room, with their eyes closed and fully engaged in chanting "Ohm's," never realized the miraculous thing that had just happened.

🌺 🌺 🌺

AFTERWORD

The Fairies' Message to Us All

The night after we became engaged, I asked Steven if he'd ever been to the headlands in Dana Point. "I've heard of it, but I've never been there," he replied.

I felt so close to Steven that I wanted to share all the secret places with him where I'd met and talked to the elementals. We drove to Selva Avenue in Dana Point and parked in the Salt Creek Beach lot. I held his hand as we walked up the sandy walk toward the headlands. The moonlight glimmered across the leaves, casting an etheric bluish-white light on the trail.

"I've never brought anyone here before," I said. "It never felt right until now." Then I pointed to a large bush. "See the face in the bush over there? See the large eyes, the nose, and the mouth? That's the face of the bush person."

I had previously discussed bush and tree people with Steven, and I knew that his shamanic studies dealt with these indigenous beings. Steven readily saw the large faces of the bush and tree people, and he felt their magical energy greeting him.

We stood under the moonlight and listened to the wind rustling. As I breathed in unison with Steven, I heard the fairies say, "*We heartily approve of this union, and we give you our ultimate blessings by bringing Steven into our midst along with you. You are both joined in the assignment of teaching custodianship of Mother Earth. Steven has been on this mission for quite some time, even preceding your own. He is an individual of considerable depth, with unique qualities of leadership, which we intend to use in the catapulting path of healing the planet.*

"*We ask that you hold love, friendship, and a spirit of playfulness in the heart of your relationship. More than anything, develop the friendship that has already blossomed with your beloved Steven. Give him room to grow, and space to breathe. Don't crowd him. Hold high expectations for both of you, and know that you have been on a Divine assignment from day one.*

"*We form a ready partnership with you and Steven, and we will be checking in with you along the way. As for the other lightworkers whose path will cross your own, you will see additional magic in your gatherings, as we fairies light the candleglow of happiness for everyone in your midst.*

"*We fairies see within the hearts of all lightworkers, and we see their sincere desire to contribute and to grow beyond their current limitations. Ask them to become involved with those of us in the elemental trenches, and we will lift their footsteps to higher reaches. We will help them expand their vision, their talents, and their circle of friendships. We will bring magic into their lives, thus giving them a heightened sense of fun and purposeful lightheartedness.*

"*Please tell people everywhere that the fairy kingdom is alive and well and living right beneath their feet! We are kindred spirits with a common purpose, and if people knew who we were and what we truly represented, they would rush to meet us in the fields, parks, and wilderness areas without delay. Please emphasize to them* that we can all put our collective hearts and minds together to reach this common goal of a cleansed and healthy Mother Earth.

"Please tell them about the power that even one person has to impact the environment positively. Please also relay the fact that we can help them heal away any factors that prevent them from enlisting in this mission—whether their fear involves the heart, the pocketbook, or the mind, we are ready and able to help them heal.

"Every time a person believes in us, we receive additional boosts of power and strength. We need these donations to fuel the big job that lies before us. Do not be afraid to believe in that which you cannot readily see. Practice these steps of taking time outside in nature, communing with us. Be aware of how you feel during these moments, and do not be afraid of being fooled by the imagination.

"We are as real as you are, and so is our love for you."

❀ ❀ ❀

(My story continues in my book *Angel Medicine*.)

Additional Resources

EarthSave International
Provides information on environmental activism, consumer information, vegetarianism, and fellowship for people interested in the environment.
1509 Seabright Ave., Suite B1
Santa Cruz, CA 95062
www.earthsave.org
(831) 423-0293 (voice)
(831) 423-1313 (fax)
(800) 362-3648 (toll free)

Laguna Yoga Essentials
Information, classes, and products related to yoga
1100 South Coast Hwy., Suite 217
Laguna Beach, CA 92651
www.lagunayoga.com
(949) 497-2022

Peter Sterling's music
www.harpmagic.com

Through Fairy Halls
A place to purchase fairy-related items, such as books, dolls, decorations, and wands
332 Forest Ave.
Laguna Beach, CA 92651
ThrufaeryHalls@cs.com
(949) 464-3891 • (949) 376-1524

People for the Ethical Treatment of Animals (PETA)
Provides assistance to mistreated animals, and serves as a resource of information about companies who are animal-friendly.
501 Front St.
Norfolk, VA 23510
www.peta.org
(757) 622-PETA (7382)
Fax: (757) 622-0457

About the Author

Doreen Virtue, Ph.D., holds three university degrees in counseling psychology. She works with the angelic and elemental realms in her writing, healing work, and workshops. Doreen teaches audience members worldwide how to hear, see, feel, and know the messages of the spirit world. She also offers a Hawaiian seminar, in which audience members get to swim with the dolphins.

Doreen has been featured on CNN, *The View, Oprah,* and other radio and television shows where she is frequently referred to as "The Angel Lady." In addition, her work has appeared in *Redbook, Glamour, McCalls, Mademoiselle,* and other publications.

If you have stories of meeting an angel or fairy, Doreen welcomes your submissions by sending them to her in care of Hay House, or to AngelStories@AngelTherapy.com. If you would like information about Doreen's Hawaiian Healing Retreats or her other workshops, please or visit www.AngelTherapy.com.

❦ ❦ ❦

Hay House Titles
of Related Interest

BOOKS

Adventures of a Psychic: *The Fascinating and Inspiring True-Life Story of One of America's Most Successful Clairvoyants,*
by Sylvia Browne

Born to Be Together:
Love Relationships, Astrology, and the Soul, by Terry Lamb

The Indigo Children: *The New Kids Have Arrived,*
by Lee Carroll and Jan Tober

The Love Book, by John Randolph Price

Visionseeker: *Shared Wisdom from the Place of Refuge,*
by Hank Wesselman, Ph.D.

AUDIO PROGRAMS

Angels and Spirit Guides:
How to Call Upon Your Angels and Spirit Guide for Help,
by Sylvia Browne

Developing Your Own Psychic Powers, by John Edward

Notes

Notes

Notes